THE STRUCTURE OF LASTING PEACE

THE STRUCTURE
OF LASTING PEACE

*An Inquiry into the Motives
of War and Peace*

By

HORACE MEYER KALLEN, Ph.D.

HASKELL HOUSE PUBLISHERS LTD.
Publishers of Scarce Scholarly Books
NEW YORK. N. Y. 10012
1974

HASKELL HOUSE PUBLISHERS Ltd.

Publishers of Scarce Scholarly Books

280 LAFAYETTE STREET

NEW YORK, N. Y. 10012

Library of Congress Cataloging in Publication Data

Kallen, Horace Meyer, 1882-
   The structure of lasting peace.

   Reprint of the ed. published by Marshall Jones,
Boston.
   1. European War, 1914-1918--Influence and results.
2. European War, 1914-1918--Peace. 3. Nationalism.
4. International cooperation. I. Title.
D610.K3 1974   940.3'14   74-1944
ISBN 0-8383-2030-9

Printed in the United States of America

To

JACOB DAVID KALLEN

My Father

A Memorial, and a Pledge

FOREWORD

TO my dear friend, Mr. George Bernard Donlin, editor of the *Dial*, of Chicago, this little essay owes its inception and completion. Early in the fall of 1917 he urged me to set down for the *Dial* these opinions of a pragmatist on the meaning of the state, its bearing on the nature and hopes of man, and on the possible future of international relations. I have done so, as well as I knew how, amid the stress and confusion of many other enterprises, each with an insistent claim on my attention. What here appears is reprinted substantially as was given to the public in the columns of the *Dial*. There is much that I should have liked, had circumstances been favorable, to have formulated otherwise, much that needs elaboration and expansion, not a little that since the essay was completed has been invalidated by events.

Its main thesis, however, stands, confirmed and strengthened. It is this: The propitious future of mankind is in the hands of the armies of the democracies and the radical and labor organizations of the world. The débâcle in Russia has denuded the present German government of the last shred of its hypocrisy. Its peace terms to the Bolsheviki, its nefarious installation and reënforcement of reaction in Finland, in Poland, in the Ukraine and in Rumania, show it set with all its power of arm and head and heart against democracy. It fears the propaganda of the Revolution more than the guns of armies, and all its peace-provisos have had in view the insurance of reaction quite as much as its own territorial and commercial aggrandizement. Its aim, in these peace agreements, has been to make the world safe for autocracy, or at least, for the existing economic and social order, with the perpetuity of exclusive national sovereignties, economic rivalries and vested interests that this implies.

This aim has its sympathizers among large and very influential classes amid the democratic powers. It has its protagonists in the governments of those powers.

Some of them, the officials of course, are inexorably dedicated to winning war, and to making the world safe for democracy, but the democracy they want to make the world safe for is that of the *status quo ante* — a democracy which differs in no very significant respect from the sort of thing the Junker and commercial classes of Germany themselves want. They see a redistribution of the territory of Europe and Asia and Africa on the basis of military advantage and economic privilege. Such a redistribution was in fact planned at a meeting of international capitalists in Switzerland at which a representative of Lloyd's was said to have participated. They see an economic war after the war by means of which their strangle-hold on the masses of mankind may be intensified. They are afraid of this new thing and terrible thing that has shown its head in Russia and that ventures so far in a programme of fundamental reform in England. They want peace soon and on any " honorable " terms, so that they may be free to guard their class-interests against the assault from underneath, an assault which the war renders swifter and more powerful with every day of its prolongation. That is said by many to be the real burden of Lord Lansdowne's now historic letter, so admirable in its demand for a *pourparler,* so significant of the unsettled and anxious mind of the more reflective among the possessing classes.

Against these class interests, which are the same among the Central Powers and the Allies, is the interest of the great masses of men, represented by the Labor and Socialist parties of the Entente countries in Europe. They see in the war the end of an old, disastrous and unjust system. They see in the war the beginning of a new national and international order, in which a genuine national democracy shall replace the capitalist establishment, and a commonwealth of nations the old system of exclusive national sovereignties. They look for initiative and leadership, over the heads of their own governments, to President Wilson. At a conference, held in London from February 19 to February 23 of the current year, they defined the war aims for democratic

Allies: — the evacuation of the occupied
territories, the complete restoration and in-
demnification of Belgium; disannexation
and a *plébiscite* in Alsace-Lorraine; the
federalization of the Balkans on the basis
of cultural autonomy and political union;
" self-determination " for the Poles, Czecho-
Slovaks and Jugo-Slavs; a Jewish state in
Palestine; the neutralization of the Dardanelles; Armenia, Mesopotamia and Arabia
under the protection of a league of nations,
the open-door in the African colonies.

Significantly, the ground and foundation
of this territorial adjustment they declare to
be a league of nations. If the Conference,
made up of representatives from England,
France, Belgium, Italy, Serbia, Rumania,
follow generally President Wilson's programme of January 8 in the matter of territorial readjustments, they follow absolutely and particularly that part of it which
deals with a League of Nations. This part
has met either with silence or empty com-
pliments or cynical comment from the governments and the Tory press of Europe.
Yet this is the part that most concerns the

future of mankind, the part that more and
more conspicuously defines the aim of the
United States in the war. It is of supreme
significance that Mr. Wilson's official and
authoritative backing on this point comes
from the representatives of the masses of
men in Europe and not the classes. It is of
extreme significance that the organized
labor group of his own country was not
represented at the Conference of these
representatives, and that the Conference
was libelled by Mr. Samuel Gompers as of
" pro-German " tendencies. It would be
interesting to know where the president of
the American Federation of Labor got his
information, an information on which this
organization failed to support the president
on just the most vital point of his foreign
policy!

To this policy the present masters of Germany have the fundamental objection that
it would undermine their mastery. Consent
to it will have to be won from them at the
point of the sword, either that of our
armies or that of their own subjects risen in
revolt, or both! To this policy the interest

of the ruling classes everywhere opposes itself sharply and distinctly. That they have
reason to fear its implications, and to fear
the leadership of its foremost protagonist,
may be seen from his address to a gathering
of New Jersey Democrats. That address
exhibits a realization of the implications of
the war for the masses of men. It speaks of
their " economic serfdom," of the hope for
them of a new day of " greater opportunity
and greater prosperity." Let the leaders of
the American Federation of Labor beware
how they answer the call of the representatives of the working classes of our Allies.
It is these who to-day " stand behind " the
president, holding up his hands and re-
enforcing his power for peace and freedom.
To refuse to work with them is to refuse to
work with him. . . .

So far, the masses of America have accepted his leadership and his programme
passively, without reflection and without
agitation. Accustomed to gauge the importance of an opinion or an event by the
headlines and editorial comments of their
newspapers, they have had their attention

distracted by these to matters more instant, more spectacular, less relevant, less fundamental. Not the kept press alone has served its masters to the detriment of the whole country, even the more or less independent journals have fallen victim of and have re-enforced the hysteria and blindness of war, have writhed and sputtered, struck out and poisoned, irrelevantly and uselessly. Yet never has there been a time when the president of the United States was in greater need of active, considered, intelligent support from his fellow-citizens who elected him to office. Opposed to his fundamental war-aims are not only the enemy we are fighting but the most powerful reactionary interests in our own land and in those of our Allies. The kind of peace we shall make will determine the kind of future we shall create for ourselves and our children. Win or lose, there is an inexorable alternative before us! On the one hand a universal and intensified nationalism, adjusted in a precarious balance of power, the power of a collection of militarized states, spending millions on munitions, perverting the minds of citizens with universal military service, economic rivalries and industrial serfdom! On the other hand a commonwealth of nations, with members free from the fear of war, free from its burdens of military service and taxation, free to convert the protest against property and privilege which has been the history of democracy to the present day into the creative and happy coöperation of mankind that has been its hope and its promise. The choice is absolute. How it will be made will be determined entirely by the degree in which a thoroughly enlightened and crystallized public opinion in America shows, by definite action taken, that it joins hands with the masses across the sea in unflinching support of the president's international programme.

H. M. KALLEN.

MADISON, WISCONSIN,
   April 2, 1918.

CONTENTS

THE STRUCTURE OF LASTING PEACE

I

INTRODUCTORY: PRECEDENT AND ADVENTURE IN THE ORGANIZATION OF PEACE

THE STRUCTURE OF LASTING PEACE

I

INTRODUCTORY: PRECEDENT AND AD-
VENTURE IN THE ORGANIZATION OF
PEACE

NEVER in the history of human warfare, which is also the history of
civilization, have the state and conduct of
war met with so much organized opposition, and so effective repudiation in principle. Wars have been fought before, and
men have before yearned and labored for
peace. But their hope of its coming and
their labor have been grounded on their
faith in supernatural intervention; lasting
peace could be God-made alone, and only
the divine miracle could end any but a
particular war with any but a particular
peace: the princes of earth are princes of
war; the heavenly prince is the prince of

peace. If to-day's war is unique in the strength of the forces engaged, the engines employed, and the blood and the treasure poured out, it is also unique in the widespread feeling that it is a civil war, in the determination that it shall be the last war, in the fact that it has been met from the outset, in all the states engaged, with organized and persistent opposition, which may be repressed or martyred, but which cannot be destroyed. Call this opposition what you will — quixotic, stupid, treacherous, foolish, saintly, what not (and at different times and in different places it may merit all these eulogia) — it remains in the bulk a unique record of the spirit in the history of the warfare of man upon earth. Precedent for it is lacking; it delineates a new feature in the aspect of humanity. It delineates a new feature because it is secular, definitive, and dynamic, while the pacifism of tradition has been theological, quietistic, and expectant. Modern pacifism rests its claim upon the ground from which militarism has immemorially worked — upon the nature and hopes of mankind. It justifies its claim by the citation of history and the analysis of social structures.

Peace foundations like that endowed by Mr. Carnegie, associations like the League to Enforce Peace, differ, however, from the vaguer groups with more adventurous social imagination, whose sentimentality is not altogether checked by perception, in that they try to study procedures and seek precedents, and aim to attain no more than they can get. They are the *realpolitiker* among pacifists, recruited mainly from the office-holding, diplomatic, and academic classes — the precedent-determined, backward-looking classes — ex-presidents, ex-secretaries of state, ex-ambassadors, professors (ex, therefore, by vocation) mostly of international law. Their influence is as obstructive to the building of lasting peace as that of the sentimental groups is irrelevant.

For the end desired has no prototype in the international relations of the past, and the situation which teaches so drastically how desirable is this end, no duplicate. It needs to be faced intelligently, on its merits, not habitually via a precedent, nor sentimentally through a rootless aspiration. What is needed to make a peace that shall endure is not a development of preëxisting relationships and conditions; these make as easily for war. What is needed is a revision of the principle on which they rest. The corpus of practices and treaties and precedents that goes by the euphemism " international law " rests in effect upon principles the exact opposite of those necessary to constitute a real international comity. There is not one of them which does not incarnate a precarious equilibrium of opposed and inimical interests, desires, and forces. War has been only the upsetting of such unsteady balances, and peace their Sisyphean restoration. To establish lasting peace there is required, therefore, the apprehension and stressing of a constitutive principle as immanent in human behavior as that which the international lawyer exploits, but making for an interlocking of powers instead of a balancing, for an international organization whose existence will not repress but set free, not frustrate but reënforce, the instinctive spontaneities and normal purposes of the so various groups of mankind.

International law has no precedent for such a means to such an end, nor can it have. What international organization existed prior to the war or now exists among the embattled alliances, has no organs to exercise such a function, nor can it have. Unities conditioned upon the menace of a common enemy can bear only an inimical relation to peace, and the alliances and combinations of powers have derived exclusively from such conditions. But there is a more basic reason for the futility of merely international precedent. States, natural though they be, none the less consist of many elements of artifice. The parts of a state are very like the parts of a machine. Their outstanding trait is rigidity. Often they perform excellently what they have been ordained to perform, but never anything more. The maiming or destruction of one part cripples the whole; no other part is able to take over its functions or to perform its services. There is no compensation, as there is in the organization of a living body. Unprecedented situations consequently tend to throw governments out of gear, to disintegrate them: their old organs cannot get adjusted to the new conditions; the governments either go to pieces, or their bureaus and departments go on doing what they have always done, and the governments are compelled to create new organs adequate to master and control the novel situation. As frequently as not the creation of new organs of government is tantamount to a revolution in the structure of the state. The Great War offers illustration of all these effects: of disintegration and revolution in the history of government in Russia; of industrial and political reconstruction in the history of government in England; of the beginning of analogous and far-reaching radical changes in the United States, of which the visible signs are the creation of the Advisory Commission of the Council of National Defence, of the offices of food and fuel production and administration, of the nationalization of railways, and of the other offices of control.

Germany, it is true, has undergone very little change, but precisely because war has brought very little news to Germany.

If these phenomena mean anything for the right definition of conditions of lasting peace, they mean that those are not conditions subject to the judgment of statesmen and diplomats, whose habits of mind and body make them inexorably deferent to precedent, tradition, and vested interests. These phenomena mean that the deciding judgment of conditions of lasting peace must be made by an enlightened public opinion, at the conclusion of the openest and freest possible discussion, in deference to the simple aspiration of the collectivities of mankind for freedom and self-expression, and with regard to the actualities that favor peace in the system of relationships into which regard for precedent has thrown the hapless rank and file of Europe. They pay the cost, theirs should be the choice. Considerations neither of precedent nor of vested interest, nor of prestige nor of honor can grasp the principle that must underly the constitution of lasting

peace, and create the organs of an international polity such that the longer they
function the surer peace will be.

The alliance of democratic common-
wealths lays claim to the discovery and
defence of this principle. With varying
stress and much confusion of counsel its
members are unanimous in declaring that
they are fighting this civil war to vindicate
it. They call it the " Principle of Nationality."

II

THE "PRINCIPLE OF NATIONALITY": "NATURAL RIGHTS" AND THE EVOCATION OF NATIONALITY

II

THE "PRINCIPLE OF NATIONALITY,"
"NATURAL RIGHTS" AND ...
...CATION OF NATIONALITY

II

THE "PRINCIPLE OF NATIONALITY": "NATURAL RIGHTS" AND THE EVOCATION OF NATIONALITY

II

THE "PRINCIPLE OF NATIONALITY": "NATURAL RIGHTS" AND THE EVOCATION OF NATIONALITY

THAT nationality is a principle is a discovery comparatively recent. Its appropriation by dynasts, by hereditary and military oligarchs, and by traders, priests, and politicians is little more recent. Nationality was a fact before it became a principle, and it was an unrecognized condition before it became a fact. Before nations were, there were dynasties or states, — that is, associations of men and women working out their lives generation after generation in service and obedience to masters whose claim to such service and obedience rested on force, tradition, and superstition. Who, particularly, these masters were, that exploited their persons and property, was a matter of indifference to the masses of Christian Europe throughout the greater part of Europe's history. And to the classes it was even more indifferent whom they exploited. Lands and people changed owners as the toll of successful military piracy or as marriage portions, and the changes were regarded as part of the necessity that is resident in the nature of things. And necessity, as everybody nowadays has been assured, knows no law.

Nevertheless, this necessity began, on the whole and in the long run, to get abrogated. Its power of constituting the nature of things began to fail. The nature of things was altering, and the force bringing about the miraculous alteration was the force of nationality. Nationality itself, however, is no miracle, no artefact. It also is an aspect and constituent of the nature of things, long merely implicit and asleep, now wakened by democracy to power and to efficacy. The awakening was slow and indirect. Remote beginnings accrue to it from the religious reformation which transferred the seat of religious authority from the head of a church to the heart of each member of the church; a nearer cause was removal of the seat of sovereignty from the head of the state to the citizenry of the state, the Puritan Revolution accomplishing this in fact in England by the trial and execution of the Cavalier king, proving thereby that the divinity which hedges about a king makes him none the less amenable to the laws of men, when men choose to assert themselves. The act was defended by opposing to the doctrine of the "divine right of kings" the doctrine of the natural rights of man, and when the French Revolution, a century and more later, repeated the act, the latter doctrine had become commonplace. Our Declaration of Independence pronounces its essence: God had created all men equal and had endowed them "with certain inalienable rights." These, as against the dynastic privilege, had come to be taken as the necessity immanent in the nature of things. Necessarily, hence, the inequalities among men — of class, of station, of privilege, of right, of property, of virtue — were contrary to the nature of things, artifices, inventions of priests and kings to perpetuate their rule. According to natural law and natural right all men are alike and all men are good; abolish class and privilege and you automatically abolish injustice and evil. So argued Rousseau, so all the eighteenth-century prophets of natural right. " You are as good as your betters, and your betters are no better than they should be. Sovereignty is everybody's and everybody is equal."

This teaching, though it may contradict the facts of life, is so near to the hopes of men, that men took it at once to heart. The Polish *shlakta,* whose indifference to the common good had made Poland the easy victim of the Prussian conspiracy against her, learned to think of the whole of Poland, even her peasantry, customs, and institutions, as the peer of her destroyers. The British colonies of North America effected their momentous revolution. The masses of France brought theirs to its epoch-making culmination. Under the inspiration of the democratic idea societies of men were acting collectively, autonomously, and with full consciousness of what they were doing, against dynasty, property, and authority, and all that these imply in cwnership and command. The beneficiaries of these took natural alarm. Prussia, Austria, Russia, England also, combined against the people of France. But only to find that their armies melted away, that their subjects everywhere celebrated the coming of the French soldier as the coming of the liberator. The republican form of government followed the French army in fact, as trade follows the flag in military-capitalistic fancy. Dynasts, anxious to maintain their prestige, found themselves compelled to defer to the free good-will of their subjects. Continental state-organization appeared to be getting turned downside up. The people were in fact becoming the sovereign.

That is, the people were not merely attaining to self-government. Nationhood, not nationality, consists of that. Nationality is a prior and a deeper thing. To say that peoples were realizing their nationality is to say that they were becoming conscious, in trying to respond to the call of the revolution, of what nature and habit and hope they and their neighbors were, and of how these were expressed in language and tradition, in memory and custom, in all that makes up a community's cycle of life. The revolutionary call to Equality meant, for the daily life, the abolition of all the caste and property distinctions that the Russians have discarded to-day. The Revolution's call to Fraternity meant, for the daily life, comradeship on an equal basis with anyone with whom communication could be effectively held — in truth with the neighbor near at hand, who speaks the same language and has the same background, who, by virtue of this sameness, *understands*. The Revolution's call to Liberty meant, first and foremost, the overthrow of the traditional oppressor at home, and the achievement there of self-government, the replacing of dynasty by commonwealth.

Had the new French nation continued to treat the peoples its armies set free as peers, as fellow-citizens, not as subjects; had Napoleon not once more restored piratical imperialism to the place from which the ideas of the Revolution had driven it, the ruling caste of Europe could never have succeeded in duping their subjects into believing in the identity of their interests and the community of their cause. Even so, their success depended on a concession to the principle that sovereignty rests in the people. For the call to resist Napoleon had to be made through an appeal to self-appreciation, through a propaganda, sometimes inspired, sometimes spontaneous, exhorting the various peoples of Europe to consider the excellence and dignity of their ancestries, their cults, their traditions, their histories, their ways of living, their arts, and particularly their languages. The most conspicuous continental instance of such a propaganda is the series of " Addresses to the German People " by the philosopher Fichte.

The outcome of this movement of ideas and events was nationality. As the doctrine that the people is the sovereign spread, it made them conscious of the quality of their life, their memories, and their institutions wherein consists their unity as a people. The need of resistance to a common foe deepened the sense of this unity, and rendered the elements which are its form objects more precious to be preserved than life itself. Among these elements a sovereign government is not to be found. A nationality is not a state, and may exist without any political separateness whatever, as do the Scotch and Welsh and Irish nationalities in England, or the Italian and French and German in Switzerland, or the Bohemian, Croat, Czech, and Serbian in Austria-Hungary, or the Ukrainian or Polish or Finnish in Russia, or the Jewish there and everywhere. A single nationality may be distributed among many states, as are the Jews and the Poles; many nationalities may compose one state, as Great Britain is composed, or Turkey, or Austria-Hungary. Nor, again, is a nationality a nation, for a nation is one or more nationalities possessed of political sovereignty forming a government resting on the active acquiescence of the governed, and animated by political purposes with regard to other nations, which it is free to carry out. Hungary is a nation; Bohemia is not; Austria-Hungary is not. England is a nation; Ireland is not. Germany is a nation; Bavaria and Prussia are not. France and Italy are nations; Russia is not. All are nationalities, plural or singular. States exist wherever government controls nationalities for its own purposes without regard to the will and preference of the nationalities. Nations exist where the purposes of government are the expression and execution of the will of the people. Nationality is the basis and material of both states and nations. It exists potentially wherever human beings are associated in durable groups, through natural, inward and spontaneously enduring media of association. It becomes actual whenever the members of the group become aware of the history and form, the cult and culture of this association, reverence its past and hope for its future.

III

THE "PRINCIPLE OF NATIONALITY": NATIONALITY AND SOVEREIGNTY

III

THE "PRINCIPLE OF NATIONALITY":
NATIONALITY AND SOVEREIGNTY

BY and large, nationality is the integration of the successive and permanent elements of group life, as personality is the integration of the successive and permanent elements of individual life. It is as useless to seek any irreducible differentia of the one as of the other. Controversy about the nature and constituents of nationality goes on, as controversy goes on about the nature and constituents of personality. Both dissolve under analysis; both are the most potent of dynamics in the making of history, which is their record. And it is upon the observation of the conditions and workings of this fact, and this alone, that a programme of lasting peace can successfully base itself. Nationality, we must always remember, is to the group what personality is to the individual: tradition is its memory; custom its habits;

history its biography; language, literature, the arts, religion, are its mind. Together these form its culture, and culture in the nationality is character in the individual. During the nineteenth century one European people after another achieved nationality simply by becoming conscious for the first time, or by recalling afresh and cherishing these items of its beings, — the Greeks, the Italians, the Germans, the various Balkan peoples subject to Turkey, the Hungarians and the Slavic races subject to Austria, the Norwegians, the Walloons and Flemings of Belgium, and the Finns and Ukrainians in Russia. The Jews have been its great exemplification from the days of Titus, the Irish since Cromwell's time, the Poles from the date of the final partition of Poland.

To-day there is hardly a single society of men in Europe, who share in the same memories and customs and speech, that has not established its nationality, and demanded for it freedom and opportunity. Where democracy prevailed the establishment took place spontaneously, as the effect of freedom; in lands with tyrannical governments it eventuated as resistance to oppression under democratic inspiration. So deep-lying is it in the funded mentality of the human families of Europe, that it has become the governing concept in a theory of civilization and a programme of life. The democratic prophet of this theory is the great Mazzini; its dynastic promulgators are Nietzsche, Chamberlain, Treitschke, von Bülow. The latter formulate it in a mythology of race, and provide by that means metaphysical and moral sanctions for German imperialism; their work, indeed, is an admirable instance of how a fact, converted into a " principle " and applied consistently and regardlessly, may become its own bitterest enemy.

Against this German misapplication of the " principle of nationality " the democratic powers oppose their own sounder formulation. But how, concretely, it applies to the present situation, its needs and demands, they have not said. What does it offer the so diverse nationalities that are the population of Europe? Which of the various components of nationality does it acknowledge as definitive? What must it safeguard and reënforce? What repress or extirpate? The Allies' declarations yield as yet no answer to these questions. They only deny the claims of imperialism, and those, only when they are German. But what is the relation of the " principle of nationality " to the imperialisms, if there be such, of England, or France, or Italy, or Russia, or the United States?

To ask such a question, any *realpolitiker* will say, is folly. The " principle of nationality " will mean at any peace conference only what the victors will let it mean, nothing more. But there are these other determinants of its meaning, nevertheless. There are the wishes and demands of the various nationalities; the implications and requirements of the fact of nationality as that appears as a force and a hope in the natural history of mankind. A lasting peace can rest only upon the harmony of all else with the latter. Now the least that can be said about the latter is that the association invoked in nationality is so pe-

culiarly intimate as to command and demand the highest degree of loyalty and
self-sacrifice from the associates. So intimate is the association that, in spite of
both criticism and evidence, the idea that
the basis of nationality is race, community
of blood and ancestry, is shared by both
democrats and dynasts. It has its propaganda even in America, in the archæologi-
cal romancing of Mr. Madison Grant and
the fictional eugenics of Mr. Seth Hum-
phrey, while in Germany the blond ancestral Aryan man-god is the most inward
shrine of the Teutomanic cult.

Scientific anthropology discounts the
whole conception, but there is envisaged in
it at least this fact — that the claim of any
large association of men to consanguinity
is an indubitable sign of a wakeful sense
of nationality. Common ancestry is indicated in the word itself, *natio*-nality, but
purity of stock can obviously not be the
basis of it. How diverse stocks, associating
together, fuse through marriage, and become of " one " blood, cannot be said. Nationality falls between race and other more

external forms of associative unity. That racial quality underlies it and is near to it, must be granted, but it is false that racial quality is identical with it. Association may spring from the original and inward nature of men, from the instinct of the herd, from a hereditary or constitutional like-mindedness; it may derive from the need of defence and offence in an unfavorable environment; it may rest upon both. Association of the first order is natural, internal; of the second order, external, artificial. The difference is as the difference between time and space. Thus, a man may change his surroundings; he cannot change his past. That is inalterable, and he is what he is because that is what that is. To abolish that, he would have to abolish himself. He may, for example, be at the same time an Irishman, a son, a father, an uncle, a cousin, a citizen, a church-member, a lawyer, a Republican, and a capitalist. Each of these words signifies a group to which he belongs. Most of them he may enter or leave without otherwise altering his nature and conditions. Others he enters without choice and cannot leave without taking leave of his life. The citizen of America may become one of England, the Baptist a Methodist, the lawyer a banker, the Elk a Mason, the Republican a Socialist, the capitalist a proletarian. But the son, father, uncle, cousin cannot cease to be these; he cannot reject the relationships these words express, nor alter them. If they obtain once, they obtain forever. So an Irishman is always an Irishman, a Jew always a Jew. Irishman or Jew is born; citizen, lawyer, or church-member is made. Irishman and Jew are facts in nature; citizen and church-member are artefacts in civilization. Natural groups, like the Irish, the Jews, or any nationality, cannot be destroyed without destroying their members. Artificial groups, like states, churches, professions, castes, can. These are social organizations; natural groups are social organisms; are, as nationalities, organisms conscious of their nature, their powers, their interests and desires, conscious, in a word, of their social personality, and acting in such a way as to preserve, enhance, and perfect it.

Empirically, then, what is affirmed in 1914 concerning *nationality* is the natural right which was declared in 1776 inalienable to *personality*. The " principle of nationality " may be stated in paraphrase of the Declaration of Independence: All nationalities are created equal and are endowed by their creator with certain inalienable rights, among them being life, liberty, and the pursuit of happiness. . . . To secure these rights governments are instituted among nationalities, deriving their just powers from the consent of the governed. . . .

That is, the principle of nationality is an extension of the scope of democracy from single to group personalities. Its application to artificial persons of the group order — corporations and the like — within the state is traditional; the struggle for its application to the nationality is only just culminating. As the declaration supplied the governing concept for the constitution of the United States, so the " principle of nationality " supplies it for the constitution of mankind. International organization,

[32]

it implies, depends upon reciprocal national responsibility, and indicates, hence, a nationhood suffrage parallel to manhood suffrage: one nation, one vote. Could this doctrine ever have been adequately applied, Europe would have had a happier history. Differences between nationalities and their corresponding states in numbers, size, wealth, quality, and power, however, weighted the influence of nations variously and unduly; encouraged in international affairs, fear, jealousy, and suspicion to such a degree that the modicum of justice and fair dealing which the United States uniquely offered Nicaragua and Mexico was looked at askance; kept international behavior set upon a policy of *laissez-faire,* which only the growing economic interdependence of the world has succeeded in modifying. The internal affairs of states, no matter how rotten, are holy, taboo to all interference. An outraged German government whines over the presumption in President Wilson's reply to the Pope's peace proposals and cannot interfere with Turkey's treatment of Armenia; the govern-

ments of our allies tread softly with regard
to one another's sacred inwards. No interference in a state's internal affairs; no
responsibility in foreign policy; no account-
ability, except to force, in anything. Each
nation, each government is *sovereign*. Each
nationality wants sovereignty. And sovereignty is irresponsibility. Sovereignty is
international anarchy.

Under the prevailing system the demands of the nationalities are just. Without sovereignty, the policy of international
laissez-faire, tempered by piratical imperialism, leaves a nationality at the mercy
of any exploiter who is stronger. Without sovereignty it fears the security of its
life, of its liberty, of its free way to happiness. Without sovereignty it is hampered
in performing what Mazzini has called
" its special function in the European work
of civilization." But this sovereignty is
also its enemy. It is the ground of international rivalry, the source of the afflatus
called " national honor," of militarism,
and of dynastic domination. The " principle of nationality " solves nothing if it

commits the post-bellum settlement to an increased number of sovereignties. It fails of its purpose if it fails to secure an open way for the spontaneous powers and happiness of nationalities. Without this security there can be no lasting peace; and under contemporary international law sovereignty both is and is not this security.

The problem of the reorganization of Europe can find its solution only in conditions that will unequivocally secure this end and just as unequivocally abolish the menace to this end which its present insurance, sovereignty, contains.

IV

NATIONALITY AND THE ECONOMIC LIFE OF STATES

IV

NATIONALITY AND THE ECONOMIC LIFE OF STATES

THE doctrine of sovereignty was a transfer of "the divinity which hedgeth about a king" from the king to the body-politic as such. It helped to protect states against the aggression of piratical dynasts, and peoples against the strengthening of their exploiters' hands from without. Interfering in the internal affairs of a state is down in the books as the international crime: internal affairs, like the Englishman's home, were a government's castle, from mediæval times taboo against entry and search. None the less, instances of international entry and search count up heavily, sometimes with good excuse and benevolent motives, as in the case of the Hay note to Rumania or some aspects of the interference of the Powers in the Balkan embroilments; mostly, however, on the pretence of guarding capital-investing " na-

tionals," or of "self-defence," or what not.
They occur in states too weak to resist —
China, Persia, Turkey, Morocco, Belgium,
Serbia. Not even America meddled with
Russia's "internal affairs," though there
was better cause than even in the case of
Rumania, and not even Russia with Austria's, though there was as good cause as
in the case of Turkey. In point of fact,
sovereignty undefended by force is empty
politically, and where an economic relation
exists between one state and another, a lie
economically.

Even with the maximum of political
reality, sovereignty cannot withstand the
undermining effect of economic enterprise,
particularly the enterprise of the modern
industrial and commercial system. This
system has automatically generated the
economic interdependence of all mankind.
Differences in basic natural resources give
the inhabitants of some parts of the world
natural monopoly of one or another raw
material that can best be converted into a
finished product in another part of the
world. There exists in the economy of

mankind a rough division of labor between the peoples of the earth. This division is dependent on their resources and their abilities, but is kept rudimentary, reduplicative, and wasteful because the community of interest which such a thing implies is restricted by governmental policies of economic particularism. These policies are partly a survival from the mediævalism of the European dynastic systems, largely a traditional privilege of interest- and rent-receiving classes. The particularism of warfare has served only to exhibit more clearly 'how contrary it is to its own needs, how doubly dependent modern states are on each other at just those points where their independence is most vigorously flaunted. For example: Indispensable engines of war require rubber, sulphuric acid, nitrates, manganese. Rubber is to be had mostly from Brazil, the East Indies, the Straits Settlements; sulphur, in commercial quantities, only in the United States, in Japan, in Sicily, and pyrites, from which it may be derived, largely in Spain; nitrates only in Chile; manganese only in Russia,

India, and Brazil. The blockade which cuts Germany off from these things cuts her off from necessaries of war, and from how many other necessaries, besides food, does it not cut her off! Her denial of international obligation can be made effective only through international obligation. Hence her demand for the " freedom of the seas " in war time. Try as she will, she cannot, in the nature of things, be a modern state and conduct a modern war, and be " self-sufficient." Nor can any other state. National economy, at least, is not sovereign. National economy, at least, means interdependence of nations.

This means that sea-rule is of paramount importance to all the states, for sea-rule is dominion of the trade-arteries, which are the life-arteries of the world, and so the greatest potentiality of victory in war and of aggrandizement in peace. This rule has been England's and it has been one of magnanimity and justice. But suppose that she had elected it should not be? . . .

Obviously, there is ground for consideration in the claim for " freedom of the seas."

The power and authority to police them ought not to rest in the interest or the whim of one state alone. Freedom of the seas is like freedom of the streets: it requires a traffic policeman and a semaphore — but the policeman must not be a law unto himself. Responsibility for the security of the international highways is international responsibility. Police power can assure guaranteed protection only when it is responsible to a democratically constituted international authority, under whose administration must come not only the ways upon the high seas, but territorially contiguous sea roads, like the Dardanelles, Gibraltar, the Suez and the Panama canals, and the harbor outlets to these ways, like Trieste, for landlocked countries, like Austria and the Balkan states (it must not be forgotten that the whole quarrel between Serbia and Bulgaria turned upon Serbia's demand of access to the sea), and for ice-bound countries, like Russia. Restriction of access, discrimination between states in the use of these ways, have defined interstate relationships and motivated policies of aggrandizement ending invariably in war. For access or control have meant exclusive sovereignty or sea power. Peace, of which the economic interdependence of nations is the backbone, can last only through the international control of international highways and terminals which this interdependence implies. Freedom of the seas means this and nothing else. It means the divorce of sovereignty from sea power.

Such a divorce would help little, however, without the coördinate divorce of sovereignty from trade and industry. The liaison of these two maintains the tariff system and requires the flag to follow the dollar. In his "New Freedom" Mr. Wilson has made a very clear statement of the evils worked in this country by "protection": how it helps to arrest industrial progress, hinders invention, initiative, efficiency; exploits workingmen and restrains the right division of labor among the peoples of the world; how it employs the profits won through the man power of this country for the exploitation of the resources and populations of other countries. And what is true of republican America is far truer of dynastic Germany or Austria or Japan. The case for free trade need not be here recapitulated, nor the fallacies of protection. What is pertinent is that protection makes for war. It seeks to create a monopoly of production or distribution which the modern economic system will not tolerate. Without tariffs the overproduction at home to undersell abroad, the scrambling for exclusive possession of foreign markets so provocative of competitive armament, the immoral division of "backward" countries into "spheres of influence" and "protectorates" — all these, and the other devices of capitalistic exploitation, would have had less chance to wreak the social and political evil they are guilty of. This evil rests, in principle, upon the use of the power and machinery of the commonwealth for the accumulation of private property by antisocial methods. Since the rise of modern industrial society capital has, to my knowledge, failed in one case only of exploitation of this rent-free privilege. This is the case of its attempt to use the blood and treasure of the American Commonwealth for private benefit of American capitalists in Mexico. President Wilson's wise and firm course with regard to Mexico constitutes an absolute break with international precedent. It warned foot-loose capital that it undertakes foreign adventure at its own risk, not the nation's. It creates precedent for the universal abolition of one constant source of international irritation. For, converted into a rule of nations, it compels capitalistic competition in undeveloped lands to stay as competition between individuals, whether personal or corporate, instead of becoming war between the states whence the capital flows.

Only a democratic victory can convert such a precedent into such a principle. States under dynastic rule, like Germany, or Austria, or Japan, or Rumania, confuse economic prosperity with personal possession. They are states in which landowners are masters (the basis of the revolution in Russia and the heart of the revolutionary programme is land-reform) without restraint, and in which the personal rather

than the social control of law and property
sustains the mediævalism of the society
whose leader is an autocrat and whose
government is a bureaucracy. The social
ideal is feudal. Its influence renders nugatory the social character which private property in modern industrial society actually
possesses, because in such states ownership
and political rule are vested in the same
persons, and government needs no sanc-
tion from the governed for its continuity.
Because the feudal order in Germany is
older and had the right of way, it is able
to make a tool of the highly modern industrial order which interpenetrates it, and is
in principle its enemy. From 1870 on, the
whole of German society was transformed
into an engine of war to be used in a programme of conquest and domination. This
programme is necessary to the security of
the ruling power, for its rule rests from its
beginnings upon its agreement to protect its
subjects against enemies in return for their
subjection. And if there be no enemies,
self-defence demands their creation. Thus
the whole Prusso-German social system de-

rives from the fiction, carefully nursed and tended, of permanent international rivalries and enmities. The dynasty's control of education has made easy the manufacture and sustenance of a popular mood in harmony with dynastic interest. German political, economic, and social theory, German history and German theology and German metaphysics have all been made, by the use of governmental favor for academic place, to expound the dogma that international warfare is the *sine qua non* of national progress, that the fulfilment of "the mission of Germany" depends upon the sword. "World power or downfall!" Rule or ruin! Not, however, nations, dynasties alone face the necessity of these alternatives, and the cry for "a place in the sun," the conception of "Mittel-Europa," the horrible animus against England are items in the dynastic struggle for self-preservation. The struggling German dynasty will continue to receive aid and comfort from the German nation so long as it can keep the nation firm in the belief that the separate and distinct interests of the two are not two, but one. And the national aid and comfort to the struggler is — sovereignty.

That the whole affair is a fiction, a somnambulism, any observer of the actual structure of the world's economy must recognize. In that structure Germany has borne a distinguished and beneficent part. Dynastic pretensions had no share in this part. It was the fruit of the scientific assiduity, the conscientious workmanship, the regard for the customer, of the German manufacturer and merchant. These gave Germany an increasingly important "place in the sun," spreading, by their excellence, not only the products of German technological superiority, but German "Kultur," in South America, in the Near East and the Far East, and in Europe and in the United States. They were welcomed, too, as an enrichment of the lives of the peoples in those parts of the world, as a reënforcement in the coöperative enterprise of civilization. The dynasty demanded, however, instead of conquest by excellence, conquest by war — possession and rule.

"That," it declares, "cannot be Germanism, which is not inherent in the German state and does not acknowledge the German ruler. The German state must hold dominion wherever there are men of German stock, and if other states and other stocks intervene, the German state must hold dominion over them." The consequences in German diplomatic and spy systems, military organization, and duplicity are notorious. Sovereignty, concentrated in a dynasty, is at once an international bully, a vicious economic programme in the shape of a tariff system, a perversion of industry from its proper function, and a trampling of weak peoples first through exploitation, then through conquest and repression.

Exploitation consists mainly in the manipulation of the external conditions of the life of a people to their disadvantage. Exploitation is hindering their free use of roads and harbors, of any means of communication without which the development of their resources is useless; it is appropriation of these resources or, where that is impolitic, discrimination against their development by means of a "protective" tariff. The second Balkan war turned on such limitations, as between Serbia and Bulgaria, and the Austro-Serb complications which precipitated the present civil war turned on restrictions as between Serbia and Austria-Hungary. Without sovereignty, that is, exclusive possession, a state is, under ordinary conditions, shut off from economic growth. The alternative has ever been — rule or ruin. In this respect, democratic states differ from dynastic ones only in degree.

There is a maxim that capital knows no nationality, that it is international, using nations simply for the purpose of exploiting other nations. Whether this be so or not, labor consciously aspires to internationality, and its aspiration is a reflex from the indisputable fact that in the economy of mankind the wealth of nations is international. As soon as this economy is freed from the repressive stress toward exclusive sovereignty, it must of its own weight and momentum, automatically, prolong peace.

For the economic enterprise is an instrument, not an end. It provides the matter of the body-politic, but not its mind. This mind is the social personality, the nationality, of a human aggregate, the product of its generous and spontaneous energies, of its free self-expression — its culture. In this a people's personality lives and moves and has its being, not in the economic order. That is undoubtedly the foundation of our house of life, but we live not in, but on, the foundations. Those exist only for the sake of the superstructure, and the firmer the base, the freer and securer the movement of those who dwell upon it. An internationalized economic order is indispensable to the liberation of nationality. The claim to exclusive sovereignty in the economic world has led to repression in the cultural. Policies of Teutonification or Ottomanization or Magyarization or Russification applied by dynastic states to subject or conquered peoples were policies of murder of social personalities. They were guided by the belief that the repression and replacement of one language and culture by another would lead to acquiescence in foreign dominion, making foreign rule easier by forced abolition of its foreignness. Nothing could have been blinder. A social personality, a nationality, resists murder as does an individual, and is infinitely harder to kill. Exploitation and even slavery are tolerated, as the non-political and non-resistant Jewish nationality has tolerated them. But it is significant that the Jewish nationality has clung to its cultural integrity and spiritually dominated its masters. So with all nationalities. Assault on spiritual values is met with immediate and powerful resistance: it is this assault that makes war between civilized peoples most of all inevitable.

Historically the assault derives from a false equation which the necessities of dynastic survival in the modern world formulate. The political state, declares the equation, is identical with its economic interests and its economic interests with its nationality. Once more we have the dogma of exclusive sovereignty. Its falsity also in this form need not be argued. We may observe the precedent and example of its contradictory in the economic history of the "sovereign states" of the United States of America, a nation of local state governments and diversified nationalities, freely associating as cultural groups, freely cooperating in the free trade of interstate commerce, its members citizens at once of the American Commonwealth and of the respective states. Time was when economic rivalry was as bitter between these states as between the European, and tariff wars and military conflict were not unheard of. But our federal system has allowed the prosperity of each state to act, as in the course of nature it had to, as a direct function of the prosperity of its fellows. There is no silly talk about "the balance of trade" between states, and other incidents of bookkeeping. The ineluctable fact of the interdependence of the "sovereign states" is incorporated into, not opposed by, the laws of the states. International commerce is only interstate commerce writ large and the problems of its control and regulation are of the same kind. The ineluctable fact of the economic interdependence of mankind must be written into the laws of nations as it has been written into those of the states. Law must declare and reënforce the fact that the foundation of national prosperity is international comity. Law must provide for equality of commercial opportunity — for equal access to undeveloped lands, to raw materials, to carriers, to harbors, to markets. Law must provide for the freedom of the highways of the world to the peoples of the world. These are the economic implications of the "principle of nationality," and so the safeguards of lasting peace.

Their attainment has for its first condition that there be banished from the council of nations any power whose existence is identified in fact as well as in assumption with a programme of exclusive sovereignty. Such an identity exists in the case of dynastic governments of rule or ruin, so that President Wilson's refusal to treat with the present German government is well-advised. But it must not be forgotten that there are others.

Let no one regard the enactment and

administration of such law as Utopian. Even *realpolitiker,* like Mr. Root, and congenital tories, like Mr. Roosevelt, will admit that in our present alliance against the murderous German dynasty necessity has forced at terrible cost what intelligence could have achieved with ease. We of America and our allies are to-day under duress of becoming avowedly what we have long been unconsciously, a coöperative economic community. We do maintain what is practically a free trade, we have pooled our carriers, we have internationalized the world's highways, we are preventing profiteering in restraint of international trade. Our commerce with our allies has become a rudimentary interstate commerce. Our economic interests are socialized, and the socialization is in effect a limitation upon the sovereignty of each state in the alliance. At the same time the acknowledgment and recognition of the social personalities, the nationalities within the alliance, is enhanced, even of Australia and Canada. That is what coöperation does. If it is an advantage for the wastage of war, what may it not mean for the creativity of peace! Its form and technique need only to be studied, perfected, and extended, to become the form and technique of the life of nations under the provisions of a democratically established peace.

V

NATIONALITY, CITIZENSHIP, AND THE EUROPEAN STATE SYSTEM

V

NATIONALITY, CITIZENSHIP, AND THE EUROPEAN STATE SYSTEM

WHEN, a year or two ago, President Wilson uttered his historic reproach of the "hyphenated American," he brought for an instant into the foreground of public opinion a little-considered quality of the existence of men which is basic to the solution of all problems of their relationships. Hyphenation is not political merely, it pervades the whole of life, increasing proportionately as civilization advances. Fundamentally it designates union and correlation, not separation, nor division. Every man is a hyphenate. Every man is the centre of an aggregate of relationships, which are normally coöperative and frequently conflicting. Every man's life is a constant compromise and choosing between alternatives so incompatible that all may not be completely satisfied at the same time. No man is, or can be, exclusively one thing and no other: son and husband, industrial baron and Christian, trust magnate and patriot, German and American, pacifist and munitions-maker, breadwinner and conscript, church-member and citizen — a man may normally be all these at the same time. Then, suddenly, he may find himself confronted with the inexorable necessity of choosing between one and another. Each implies reciprocal rights and duties, each makes insistent and clamorous claims. Which shall be granted, which denied, instinct, tradition, habit, fear, imitation, standards of class and rank determine far more than intelligence. Yet at no point than in such choices is intelligence more needful or significant.

What is important about the hyphenation of mankind is the classes into which it divides. Men are hyphenated by nature and by art. The relationships involved in the former are congenital and inalienable, internal to a man's character and coincident with his existence. The relationships involved in the latter are acquired or assumed; external to a man's character and existence, alienable, and not indispensable. Nationality is, we have seen, a hyphenation belonging to the nature of things; vocation, religion, citizenship are hyphenations created in the process of history. Men are born English or Jew or Chinese, and their association with men similarly born is involuntary and spontaneous. Men become farmers or carpenters or physicians, Christians or Mohammedans or Judaists or Buddhists, citizens of Russia or France or America, and their association with men similarly preoccupied is voluntary and directive, governed by considerations of advantage and the forces of circumstance. These associations men pass into and out of at need, or pleasure, or both. The others they cannot but remain in until they die. It is for the sake of those others, indeed, that vocation and religion and the state arose; to liberate their powers and to elaborate and enrich the idiom of their existence. Much of the trouble of civilized society derives from the fact that these artificial associations have overturned what they should have sustained, that they have changed from tools of living into purposes of life, that they have become idols.

This is to-day even truer of economic and political associations than it was in the Middle Ages of the religious association they have replaced. Capital and the State are the idols of modernity, and the two are, as we have seen, so interpenetrated that the worship of the one implies the worship of the other, even in democratically constituted states. I do not mean by this to deny that the economic order is at the foundation of civilized society. I mean merely to assert again the always obvious and always ignored truism that the economic order presupposes a community not economic, which this order serves, and that modernity's elaboration of it inconceivably beyond the effective gratification of human needs is unnecessary, and indeed inimical, to the free life of mankind. In so far as this civil war which German dynastic interest has thrust upon the world seeks justification from the equating of economic advantage and political sovereignty with nationality, it seeks justification from a lie. In fact, the whole modern system of economic rivalries, supposedly inevitable under the "law of diminishing returns," is due to the misappropriation of economic endeavor to dynastic and capitalistic uses; is due to the militarist requirement of a "self-sufficient" state. Just and free conditions of economic endeavor break this law. As Simon Patten has shown, variation of uses and extension of consumability not only keep returns at par or increase them; they also multiply the "division of labor" and so generate coöperative interdependence. The competitive politico-economic system, with its tariffs and other dishonesties, rests upon *sameness* of economic enterprise; the greater the differentiation, the less the rivalry. States that grow and make different things, that vary their use and bring them constantly within the easier reach of more and more people, become more and more dependent on each other with time. Germany's rivalry with England did not spring from the diversity of the two states' products, but from their identity. The latter made them competitors; the former, friends.

Now the unnecessary existence of rivalry is a perversion of function in state and industry. These, it must be remembered, are tools, not ends. To use them democratically is to use them in behalf of the freeing and enhancement of inward and spontaneous differences, not of their repression. The most we can mean by law and justice and equality of opportunity is such an arrangement of the material upon which human life nourishes itself as will permit and extend the freest development, expression, and interplay of human individualities. Upon those and upon those alone are the essences of civilization and culture grounded and grown. And in those, nationalities interpenetrate and support each other. National genius requires an international soil and sustenance. The music, literature, painting, sculpture, and philosophies of peoples, their religions, and even their preëminent sciences are the most precious, the most excellent, the best known, and most honored, and yet the most intimate and national of their achievements. Yet their substance and source are the most wide-ranging and diversified. For these, things of the spirit, protection is destruction; free-trade, strength. English Shakespeare is nourished upon the Italian Renaissance; German Goethe (he avows it vehemently, again and again), upon English Shakespeare. Each is the declared national superlative of nationality and each is superlatively hyphenated. The supremacies of the other institutions of national culture are similarly international. Indeed, culture, of both the nation and the individual, is hyphenation. That is why the highest excellences are achieved by the more democratic peoples or the more democratic times, or both — fifth century Athens, Augustan Rome, the city-states of Italy and Flanders, England from the eighteenth century on, France in the nineteenth century, Germany from the birth to the death of Goethe. For democracy, more basically than anything else, is hyphenation. Since the one and only thing democracy can mean is the sympathetic understanding of the other fellow, with his different origin, nature, background, and outlook, and the free and coöperative recognition of his right to be and to thrive. Democracy, like humanism, is the mind's reverence of, and the heart's sympathy for, individuality, and individuality never occurs except in nationalate form. Men are always Englishmen, or Chinamen, or Frenchmen, or Germans, and so on; they are never merely men. Nationalities are the roots, and national cultures the fruits, of trees of human life whose soils are the economic and political systems that feed or starve them. These systems are not inherent parts of the nature of nationalities; they can be and are artificially altered without hurt to men. Nationalities cannot be.

What I am trying to say is this: The world's politico-economic establishments are needful guarantees and conditions of nationality, but not its constituents. Democratic progress in such establishments would provide for nationality the same fortune as is religion's. In the record of civilization religion is the first free manifestation of nationality. The cities and states of antiquity are distinguished primarily by their cults and their patron divinities, and the divinities have a direct or indirect ancestral connection with their worshippers — Athene for Athens, Phœbus for Sparta, Jehovah for Jerusalem. In the Middle Ages, cities and states are distinguished by their patron-saints — St. George for England, St. Denis for France. Catholicism did not in fact designate universality of cult; it designated, and does still, a local and national and vocational particularism, with a general mythology and theology for background. Religious imperialism, for which Catholicism is a euphemistic synonym, is the attempt to compel universal conformity in religious matters. The history of that attempt is the darkest in the whole dark record of mankind — from the torture and slaughter of heretics within the church, the extermination of Lollards and Hussites and other dissidents, the persecution of Jews, the assault upon Mohammedans, to the terrible religious wars of the Reformation. Modern Europe begins with the mediæval assumption of the identity of church and state, the church using the state to enforce religious conformity. The Middle Age is the period of religious imperialism. With the Protestant Reformation this imperialism is shattered, to be followed by religious nationalism. States disable dissenters with the infinite variety that the ingenuity of the creed-monger is so distinguished for. In Protestantism sects multiply, however, and the alternative to tolerance is anarchy or rebellion. Hence little by little the absolute divorce between church and state which political theory advocated from the beginning gets achieved in the compromises of political practice. What helps more than anything else to secure this end is the steady secularization of mankind by the substitution of humanitarian, scientific, industrial and æsthetic interests for the religious ones, so that finally citizenship is altogether detached from adherence to a special confession. The establishment of tolerance was the establishment of democracy in the sphere of religion, the application of the principle of "live and let live" to associations whose differentiæ were varying declarations about the unseen and its bearing upon the destiny of man. How deep the roots of such associations lie, may be gathered from the fact that so vehement an Americanist as Mr. Roosevelt is still a member of the Dutch Reformed Church. In this respect, as in many others, this ex-president, quite like other men, is still a hyphenate, and it is, on the whole, the irrelevance of this form of hyphenation to the actualities of his life that keeps it from creating a momentous option for him. And for all men, in our Christian civilization, save, perhaps, those who are Catholics, and owe allegiance to the Pope. For with Protestantism there began a secularization of the world which more and more drove the religious concern from the centre to the periphery of human interest. Under the new and growing conditions of tolerance and freedom sects multiplied, yet no one was the worse. The secular mood simply changed the rôle of religion back from an idol of life into a tool of living. Its connection with the state was severed and the power by means of which it was compelled to struggle for existence altered from physical force to moral excellence.

The place left vacant by religion was filled by nationality. Nationality is the secular aspect of the same self-conscious pride of social personality of which religion is the first utterance. In backward and mediæval states the two still interpenetrate and imply each other; their criteria are doctrines of especial consideration from divinity and a special predestinate service to execute on behalf of God. Germany, we are instructed, is a chosen people with a mission, boasting a state-religion beside which dissident sects are at a disadvantage. Free states, on the contrary, have no room for either doctrine. They have permitted the sinister connection of state and church to fall into desuetude, or have violently severed it, or have taken measures to prevent its arising. Now underneath nationality, as underneath the religions of antiquity, there lies, as we have seen, an actual or hypothetical consanguinity of the individuals nationally associated, a hereditary inward similarity whose outward manifestation is the community and culture of the associates. Clearly, the connection between political establishment and nationality is as unnecessary and minatory as that between state and church. The present civil war is the price mankind is paying for the modern error even as it paid for the mediæval error. How little necessary the connection is between nationality and the state the history of nationalism itself shows, no less than the actual organization of various states — Switzerland with her French and Italians and Germans, Great Britain with her English and Welsh and Scotch and Irish, Belgium with her Walloons and Flemings, the United States with all the nationalities of the world associated in the common American citizenship.

Nationality, in a word, is as independent of citizenship as religion. A citizen is associated with his fellows in a state for political purposes. These purposes are to guarantee to individuals and to groups, as our Declaration of Independence asserts, life, liberty, and the pursuit of happiness.

Disentanglement of the state from religion has made it the guarantor of religious freedom. The next step in the liberation of mankind must be to detach it completely and everywhere from nationality that it may become the guarantor of national freedom, enfranchising the inner life of nationalities for creation and self-expression in the world of culture as it does sects in the realm of religion. That this is more and more the case in countries with free and responsible institutions need not be argued. But if peace is to become lasting, it must be made everywhere and equally the case.

And there's the rub. Even in the United States, in the very face of the facts of the daily life, men labor under the superstition of the identity of nationality with citizenship, and the fanatical devotion to nationality among the Jugo-Slavs, the Irish, the Poles, the Lithuanians, to say nothing of the Germans, is certain, if peace be not made on the basis of an absolute divorce between citizenship and nationality, to maintain the war-creating system of international disorganization. Democracy, on which peace ultimately depends, demands this divorce. Without it, the German conception of the state, particularly effective for wartimes, is bound to prevail. According to this conception the state is the be-all and end-all of existence, greater than society and inclusive of it. Neither individuals nor groups have being or significance outside the state. They exist by its sufferance and live for its service. It is the Sole Individual, the great Whole, the synthesis and fulfilment of all human associations, antedating and superseding them, prior in existence and in right. Precisely opposite is the democratic view. Democratic states are pluralistic. For democracy, political association is not primary, but secondary; not the synthesis of other associations, but one type added to the others, and maintained only so long as it effects the special purpose for which it was created. Its authority rests upon the "consent of the governed," is never absolute, never infallible. There is appeal from it, even, as John Locke says, "to heaven." He means that the right to rebel against bad government is inalienable, that the people are the sovereign, and *all* the people.

When, therefore, states have failed, they have done so invariably because the power of government has been used by and for a part, against the whole of a people: in autocracies and oligarchies, by minorities against majorities; in democracies, by majorities against minorities. In this way the function of government, which is like that of the traffic police, so to keep the ways of life open that each traveller may have equal opportunity with his fellows to journey unhampered to his goal, becomes perverted and the law substitutes favoritism for equity. Of the "law of nations" this has been particularly true. The system of state sovereignties is answerable for all the forms of imperialism that derive from nationalistic aggression — Germanification, Magyarization, Ottomanization, and so on, with all that such programmes imply in the economic and political orders. Unless an international is substituted for this national system, the world will never be safe for democracy. To speak of a few cases in

Europe alone: there are Magyar and German minorities in Bohemia and in the Austrian territory claimed by Rumania, just as there is a great Slavic majority in the Hungarian dominion; two-thirds of the Macedonia claimed by Serbia is inhabited by men of Bulgarian nationality; Alsace is largely " German "; a proportion of Poland is Jewish, Lettish, Lithuanian, Ruthenian. A settlement according to "the principle of nationality" which would effect only a change in hegemony would have Europe at war again in less than a generation. Minorities must be safeguarded even as majorities must be freed if peace is to last, and minorities cannot be safeguarded without international guarantees that will once and for all divorce citizenship from nationality. Of course, such guarantees would constitute a comprehensive easement on the European system of state sovereignties and would require a simple and strong machinery to make them effective.

VI

SOME PROBLEMS OF READJUSTMENT: POLITICAL BOUNDARIES AND NATIONAL RIGHTS

VI

SOME PROBLEMS OF READJUSTMENT: POLITICAL BOUNDARIES AND NATIONAL RIGHTS

VI

SOME PROBLEMS OF READJUSTMENT: POLITICAL BOUNDARIES AND NATIONAL RIGHTS

"NO annexations, no contributions, no punitive indemnities" has become a familiar formula for the settlement of the war's issues, dear to the hearts of doctrinaire political radicals and to the minds of sentimentalizing pacifists. Its generality and vagueness are the best of its endearing virtues. It is as unreflective, as unregarding of the concrete and specific constituents of an organization of democratic peace as the formulæ of the pan-Germanists among the Central Powers or the panic-Americans and bitter-enders, like Colonel Theodore Roosevelt and Bolo Pasha, among the democracies of the Entente. The notion on which the latter advocate their readjustment is the notion of *vae victis*, and for the Junkers of Germany nothing could be more apropos to keep the people of Germany at war in the Junker interest. The notion which guides the anti-annexationists is in effect that of the *status quo ante*, and that is only just less desirable to the irresponsible German governing class than German victory. The formula against annexations, contributions, and indemnities really looks backward. It denies to the war the salutary consequences in the reorganization of mankind which alone can a little mitigate its horror. If acted upon, it would in a generation bring on a new war with the same motives in play as in this one. Regarded squarely, it is a piece of what William James used to call vicious abstractionism, generated without consideration of the specific situations and living problems it is intended to relieve and to settle; situations and problems which, moreover, have themselves so changed in character and implication since the beginning of the war that the bearing of any formula upon them, including the formulæ of democracy and nationality which dominate these studies, requires a constant and watchful readjustment that renders a priori assumptions of any sort venturesomely speculative.

Assumptions, however, must be made, and their danger is lessened in the degree in which they utter the enduring motives in human nature and social action. In the light of these, as well as in view of the originating conditions and purposes of the present war, a lasting peace cannot be a negotiated peace.

A lasting peace must needs be a dictated peace, and the dictator's victory must needs be at least so thoroughgoing as to compel, should it be found desirable, those members of the Central-European establishment whose policy is responsible for the atrocities on the high seas, in Belgium, in France, in Poland, and in Armenia, to stand public trial for murder. Peace without this degree of victory is too likely to be only an armistice: students of ancient history may recall the "negotiated" peace of Nikias between Athens and Sparta during the Peloponnesian war, a peace that served only to prolong the intolerable agony of the noblest family of mankind that antiquity knew. Even a German peace would be better, because more enduring, than a "negotiated" one and a German peace would mean submission to the German hegemony over civilization. It would mean this even if the government of Germany were well-intentioned toward mankind. It would mean this because outside of the regions of sentimentality and dialectic might is right. It would mean this because history is the record of claims and privileges of the few over the many yielded by the many to force, deferred to through custom, and finally revered and idolized through old age. The claims and privileges of dynasties and churches and fortunes are the most notorious instances, and the less conspicuous ones are infinite. International democracy will have to be established by force and sustained by force, before it becomes naturalized in the economy of civilization by education, self-sustaining through habit, and finally sacred through immemorial old age. Even national democracy, it must be remembered, is a very young and tender plant in this millennial civilization of ours, a plant not yet quite secure even in countries where it sprang fully panoplied from the heads of the Fathers. Force alone can replace anarchy in international relations by law, even as it has done so in personal relations. Whether that force be military, or of another specification, is indifferent. The illusion that in personal relations "right is might" derives from the fact that the might which sustains the right that is might is not so visible in those relations as in the relations between states. Right is might only by the force of the collective pressure of society toward this "right." The rule of law is the rule of the largely unseen, but the ready and watchful power of the state whose visible symbol is the policeman on his beat.

Hence, lasting peace is to be grounded upon two postulated events. First, a democratic victory with the permanent maintenance of sufficient organized force, whether military, or economic, or both, to keep secure the fruits of this victory. Secondly, such definition of the settlement and such use of the insuring force as to invigorate and expand the creative instrumentalities that are inevitably making for the internationalization of mankind. These instrumentalities have gone, in our survey, by the names democracy and nationality. And the significant thing about them is that they are ideals even more than they are instrumentalities.

There exist, however, within the councils of the Entente itself strongly entrenched interests unwilling to consider a settlement in terms other than those of the traditional diplomatic piracy. Between the luckily abolished Russian bureaucracy and France and England, between Italy and these powers and Rumania and these powers, agreements existed which if carried out would have led to a new war within less than a generation, agreements altogether counter to the announced fundamentals for which England and the United States entered the war. Happily, events have taken the issue from the hands of intriguing diplomacy in Russia, and President Wilson, speaking for the people of the

United States, is determined to keep un-
sullied the record of our country in this
crisis in the affairs of mankind. But a
traditionally ordained residuum remains,
like the commercial "war after the war,"
and the land-grabbing claims of the various lesser allies of the Entente, and the
claims of its numerous protégés — the
"small nations" of Europe, Poles and
Letts and Lithuanians and Jugo-Slavs and
Ukrainians and Finns. These clamor for
their establishment as sovereign states with
all that this implies. Each of them has at
its mercy minorities of other nationalities
whom it bitterly opposes, the attitude of the
Polish nationalists toward the Jews leaving
nothing to be desired even by a Prussian
lieutenant in ferocious cruelty. The problem of readjustment is at bottom the
problem of reconciling these counter-claims,
of redefining the post-bellum economic programme and the actual territorial lusts of
the major powers in harmony with the
principles of democracy and nationality.

It has already been indicated how completely these principles controvert the

traditional assumptions of exclusive state-sovereignties from which international "law" and diplomatic deviation derive; how they utter the more deep-lying conditions and forms of the organization of Europe — those that are so obvious that they go unnoticed save when an assault upon them is made. What they point to, in the post-bellum reorganization of mankind, is far less a shifting of ante-bellum boundaries than a redefinition of the rights and duties pertaining to peoples living outside as well as within those boundaries, in their relations to one another. At no point on the map of Europe are ethnic coincident with political boundaries. The political nationalism which seeks to create these coincidences, thus multiplying the number of irresponsible sovereignties, is as vicious as it is blind. It seeks merely to multiply the type of situation in which this civil war began. The festering areas of this situation were, of course, the Balkans, where the conflicts were in play of the Balkan peoples with Turkish dominion, of Serbian economic necessity with Bulgarian national confraternity, of Serbian national sympathy with Austro-Hungarian economic greed, and of the group and personal aspirations of all these peoples with German economic greed and cultural paranoia. War only universalized and dynamified these conflicts. Under the political system of independent state-sovereignties, it was unavoidable.

Where, however, the principles of democracy and nationality operate, the state is not, it will be remembered, the paramount and all-compelling social organization. It is one, among many others, coordinate with them, and serving a very definite and highly specialized function with regard to them — the function of umpire, of regulation and equalization, in the issues that arise between them. In terms of its function the state is an administrative area, not a cultural nor a racial one, and the problems and technique of administration are constituted of quite other considerations than those of race and culture. These others, and these alone, have any claim to enter into the definition of political boundaries, and they are reduceable to just one — the scientifically ascertainable limits of administrative efficiency in view of the economic and cultural interdependence of mankind. The geography of an area, the relation of its contiguous nationalities to waterways and harbors and railways are much more significant for the happiness of these nationalities in their political correlations than any form of racial hegemony. Thus, the unity of the British Empire is functionally of a very different kind from the unity of the United States of America or of the Austro-Hungarian Empire. Great Britain's colonies and provinces, peopled by her own nationalities, have a tremendously completer independence than America's constituent "sovereign" states; Austria's Hungary has the sovereignty, and more, of Britain's Canada; Austria's Bohemia, that of an American state; her Bosnia none at all. The constituent nationalities of Russia, prior to the revolution without any sovereignty whatsoever, are now aiming at complete political independence regardless of all other considerations, regardless, that is, of the very conditions on which their national lives must be built.

Now political experience makes, on the whole, against the small nation-state. It is always quarrelling with its equals and an object of desire to its superiors. Its sovereignty rests on sufferance, even with "international guarantees" (occasion turns these into "scraps of paper"), and its prosperity is a provocation. Experience would create quite other satisfactions, for the claims of the Entente's protégés, than political sovereignty. The case of the Jugo-Slavs is here the crucial, the test case. These eight or more varieties of the Slavonic species have all the traits of nationality. Among them the Serbo-Croats are politically the most significant and culturally the most self-conscious. They constitute, indeed, ethnically, as well as otherwise, a single nationality. Their political entanglements have precipitated the war. They are citizens in the two sovereign states Serbia and Montenegro, and subjects in the Magyar dependencies of Bosnia and

Herzegovina. The programme of political nationalism would combine these areas into a greater Serbia under the present Serbian ruling house. The Montenegrin king is naturally reluctant to surrender his dynastic prerogative, and is said, in spite of his acquiescence, to be flirting with Austrian nuntios. The Berlin-Buda-Pesth financiers, again, and the promoters of Mittel-Europa, cannot imaginably relax their grip on Bosnia and Herzegovina. In the conduct of the Hungarian rulers toward their Slavonic subjects Prussianism had a perfect incarnation. This conduct is to be sharply distinguished from that of the Austrians toward their Slavonic fellow-citizens. The former is far more a model of frightfulness than Prussia in Alsace and Lorraine; the latter manifested the wise statesmanship that distinguished England's relations, since the Boer war, to her dependencies. Francis Ferdinand, the murdered archduke, planned to extend the Austrian policy to the whole of the Dual Kingdom. Rumor will not down that his murder was arranged in Berlin and Buda in order to prevent the federal coördination of all the nationalities in the empire, a coördination which would have made the way toward Mittel-Europa a difficult one indeed, and would have deprived the politico-nationalist Serbo-Croats of their most dynamic motive. The present emperor, it happens, is even more set upon this coördination than the late Archduke. His plans and hopes, neither suit junker Germany nor nationalist Slav. His plans and hopes, however, whether through self-interest or intelligence, are in harmony with the geographical and economic determinants of the fate of all the nationalities herein involved, the independent states of Serbia and Montenegro included. These states have undergone wars for the sake of railways and access to the sea. Those desirables, and many more, may come to their people by a political union with Austria-Hungary. Such a union would be a violation of the formula "no annexation"; but if it is a union on a democratic basis, under effective guarantees, it becomes as true that Austria is annexed to them, as they to it.

Such guarantees, however, require a rad-

ical change in the constitution of the Dual
Monarchy, a great easement upon its sovereignty. They would need profoundly to
alter the incidence of taxation, the scope of
suffrage, and the conditions of cultural and
religious organization. Even with the very
desirable creation of the wished-for Greater
Serbia as a part of the new Austrian Commonwealth of politically equal nationalities,
the guarantees could not be merely written
into the law of the land alone. To be effective, they would have to be trans-national,
enforcible by international intervention.
Prescription is futile without enforcement,
as the notorious example of the much-
chastened and newly enlightened Rumania
shows. Under the provisions of the treaty
of Berlin which established this dynastic
and landlord-ridden state (now striving
nobly and with heroic effort toward democracy, economic as well as political),
Jews, on whom the Rumanian political
mediævalism bore even harder than on the
Rumanian peasant, were to be established
in citizenship equally with their fellow-
countrymen. Rumanian legislation ren-

dered these provisions completely nugatory. The taboo on "interference in a state's internal affairs" kept the Jews from appeal and redress. The Jewish minority was and is completely at the mercy of the non-Jewish majority. The war has led the Rumanian government of its own motion to plan to remove this tragic injustice, but had there existed an international authority with power to enforce its verdicts, to which the minority or the powerless could have appealed, the history not only of the Jews but of the downtrodden peasants of Rumania might have been otherwise written.

In a readjustment such as the basic needs of their peoples show as wisest for Austria-Hungary and her Slavic subjects and Slavic rivals, the lesson is obvious. The geographically and economically defined administrative area which may be the state of Austria-Hungary-Serbia, would be much larger than the original. The state would be a democratic coöperative commonwealth of nationalities with their social and cultural differences strengthened and enhanced by their economic and political unity. To secure this, however, to turn what is written as a law into what is practised as a life would require a superior authority to which endangered minorities could appeal and from which they might actually get justice.

As with Austria-Hungary, so with Russia and her constituent nationalities, with Turkey and hers, with France and Alsace-Lorraine, with the other Balkan states. The chief problem in a readjustment that shall be advantageous to the masses of men rather than to political or economic hegemonies and other vested interests is the problem of creating a machinery that shall effectively safeguard the rights of minority nationalities to life and liberty and the pursuit of happiness. Without such a machinery exclusive sovereignties, and wars, are inevitable. With it the nullification of international obligations becomes in the long run impossible, and the whole political programme based on the present state-system irrelevant. The quarrels will fall to the ground that have arisen among Poles over dragooning the unwilling Galicians, who have in recent years been perfectly well off with Austria, into union with their unspeakable chauvinist fellow-nationals of Russia, who have learned nothing from history and remain as intolerant and piratical as the Shlakta whose selfishness and sensualism destroyed the Polish state. And so the quarrels of the Ukrainians, the Ruthenians, the Finns, and others with the Russians. So, quarrels anywhere between nationalities. Once democracy, in accord, of course, with the living law, and the enduring moods of a people, is prescribed for an economico-political area, and minorities in such an area are safeguarded by the proper machinery of law, the creative and coöperative tendencies in human nature and the compulsion of the industrial machine will, other things being equal, automatically and without restriction effect the indefinite duration of peace.

VII

SOME PROBLEMS OF READJUSTMENT: CONTRIBUTIONS AND INDEMNITIES

VII

SOME PROBLEMS OF READJUSTMENT: CONTRIBUTIONS AND INDEMNITIES

THAT the formula, "no contributions, no indemnities," is sound economics anybody is bound to acknowledge who has read Mr. Norman Angell's trenchant and convincing dissipation of the "great illusion." But that it is sound psychology is itself an illusion. If it were sound psychology, wars would never be waged by nations, nor murders and thefts committed by men. In the long run both are foredoomed to economic failure and social scorn. Both recur, nevertheless, with such constancy and so typically as to be institutional to civilization. When defining the place of contributions and indemnities in the foundation of lasting peace, therefore, it becomes more needful to regard their indirect influence on the mental states of the nations between whom they are to pass, than their direct influence upon national economies.

Now it is significant that the formula against indemnities and contributions is a democratic and socialistic formula. It is sounded in Russia and the United States and England, but it is barely echoed in Germany. And it comes from the mouths of those who are preoccupied with economic, not psychological, relationships. In terms of the latter, contributions and indemnities are of the same type of thing as the pinch and blow of the childish bully. They constitute jointly and severally an immediate gratification of the sense of superiority, of the lust for power, regardless of future consequences. They belong to the intoxicants, and although specious ratiocination may give the demand for them the appearance of a policy, they are, if history is to be trusted, the most impolitic thing a conqueror can undertake who wishes to hold his conquests with ease and permanence. "Frightfulness" is merely a nearer and directer view of the gratification of the same lusts.

The problem of contributions and indemnities is at bottom the problem of the

control and extirpation of these lusts. No
doubt the democracies allied against Germany have them, but precisely because
they are democracies, the lusts have their
own counterpoise in the national mental
states: the creation of the formula about
contributions, indemnities, and annexations
is itself sufficient proof. The lusts are most
constitutional to Germany. German rule
in Belgium and northern France, for example, has consisted of resurrecting and
applying the imperial malpractice of the
piratical empires of antiquity. This usage
has established, in the attitude of the inhabitants of these lands, in their emotional
set, a hatred toward Germany that is deep-
rooted and permanent. Nothing short of
complete extermination can mitigate the
blood-feud which has been created by the
use of the levy and the *corvée,* by the wanton
and malicious destruction of property and
of the self-respect of women and men. Any
plan looking toward the permanent holding
of these territories by Germany, or in case
of their evacuation, any friendly relations
between their governments and that of Ger-

many after the war, would — had it been guided by considerations of advantage and the lessons of history instead of sadistic vainglory — have required a policy precisely the opposite of that adopted, particularly in the very beginnings of the occupation. The conspicuous absence of such a policy is symptomatic, and the terms of peace must be such as to remove the causes of the symptom. These causes are the German ruling class and the system of education they imposed upon the German masses.

There are, hence, two sets of considerations for the peace conference to heed in the financial adjustments between the German government and people and the democratic powers. The first of these is of reparation for goods stolen and damage done. All levies should be returned, with interest at an appropriate rate. All forced labor should be paid for, at twice the market rate, because it was forced, with interest at an appropriate rate. For the murder of helpless civilians there can be no adequate compensation, but their dependents should receive a pension at the hands of the German nation. All property wantonly destroyed should be paid for, with an additional contribution for the absolute loss involved.

The foregoing stipulations apply to matters individual and private, and the obligation of the Germans on both fronts is not without its analogue in the obligations of the Russians in the East. The Germans, it is to be remembered however, are the aggressors. Damage done is the direct consequence of their initial and malicious act. There is a type of fundamental damage to which the technique of modern warfare compels the defenders also to contribute. Such is the damage suffered by the terrain of Champagne. The soil of that once beautiful and prosperous region has been literally shot away. Its subsoil is chalk, of the same formation as the unbearing chalk-cliffs of England. The latter have been barren from time immemorial, and the whole Champagne region is likely to be so henceforth. Should this prove to be the case, France has suffered a fundamental damage, one that means for her an altered economy after the war. For this damage full payment is impossible, but that payment should be required, sufficient at least to ensure life and health and security to the natives of the region while their government helps their lives into new channels, seems not only just, but indispensable. What that payment should be could of course be told only by a body of geological and economic experts.

Payment for such and the other damages reviewed above would be in the nature of reparation. And for reparation the German people as well as the German government is responsible. The people is responsible because the whole nation assented to the government's aggression. The enormous war tax of 1913 was indispensable to the German government for its secret preparations for its assault upon mankind in 1914. This tax could never have passed the Reichstag without the vote of the Socialists, which it got. In that vote the whole German people were committed to the war-party, anti-militarism and internationalism were betrayed. By that vote all Germans share the obloquy and responsibility of their government for thrusting civil war upon civilization. But they share it also for its treachery and cruelty in the conduct of the war. They share it because their representatives in the Reichstag raised at no time and under no circumstance any significant voice against the policy of "frightfulness" of the political and military leaders. That not even the dissident among the Socialists uttered such a protest is testimony to the extraordinary grip of the government upon the fears and hopes of its subjects.

Its grip on their fears is obvious enough. Its grip on their hopes would have been impossible without its thoroughgoing and programmatic use of the nation's educational system for its own especial purposes. By its almost absolute control over education, a control the only parallel for which is that exercised by the priesthood over the Catholic's education, the government succeeded in keeping the people of Germany subjects of a dynasty when they should have been citizens of a state. By virtue of its control of education the German government is a *cause* of the iniquity of the German people, instead of one among other constituents in that iniquity. According to some thinkers, its control of education makes it the chief, if not the only, cause. Now the elimination of this causal power from the government of Germany is the second of the two sets of considerations in the financial readjustments between that government and the democracies of the Entente. This set of considerations demands the annihilation — in fact, only a little more in Germany than elsewhere — of governmental control of education. Annihilation may be accomplished in two ways. First, educational institutions can be rendered completely autonomous (a consummation devoutly to be desired everywhere) at home. Secondly, as many as possible of the German youth can be educated abroad.

For the second method the democratic use of indemnities offers precedent. The precedent derives from the relations between the Western powers and China, and its application — in the form established by the United States — to their relations with Germany cannot but be liberal and liberating. When the Western powers exacted from the quite helpless Chinese government and people indemnities for the damage done by the Boxer rebellion of which this government and people was a victim even more than they, the United States alone, of all the powers, directed the application of its share to defraying the expenses of educating young Chinese in America. Let the democratic powers follow this precedent with regard to the government of Germany. Let the terms of peace require that one young German out of every thousand, both men and women, shall from his or her twelfth year on be educated abroad — in the United States, in England, in France, in Italy, or in Russia. An indemnity should be required to defray the cost of so educating the new generation. The money of this indemnity ought not, however, to be raised by taxes from the German people. It ought to consist of a trust-fund, created by confiscating all the properties of the royal families of Germany, and of the great German landlord class, the junkers. This trust might be held and administered by an international educational commission for the good of mankind.

There are certain desirable extensions of this procedure to other governments that I shall discuss in connection with the organization of peace. At present I am concerned only with its influence on the mental set of the government and people of Germany. An indemnity so specified as the foregoing should be satisfactory to liberals as well as conservatives in the matter of war-settlements. It obviously can work no injustice upon the people of Germany. Rather is it a service to them, deriving as it does, not from taxation, but from the appropriation to public use of the property of their exploiters and masters. It is bound to set them free from one of the most potent instrumentalities of this mastership. Upon the minds of the masters, on the other hand, it is bound to impress the fact that they have been whipped in the only language that they, like bullies everywhere, are capable of understanding. It is bound to go a long way toward converting the bully into a peaceful citizen, for the expropriation of the propertied classes cuts the ground from under their arrogance. While, again, participation, through its educated men, in the life and labor of other peoples, leads the citizenry of a land to respect and understanding for these others.

VIII

THE EQUALITY OF NATIONS BEFORE THE LAW AND SOME OF ITS IMMEDIATE PREREQUISITES

VIII

THE EQUALITY OF NATIONS BEFORE THE LAW AND SOME OF ITS IMMEDIATE PREREQUISITES

SAY about victory and annexations and indemnities and contributions all that can be said, and you are no nearer a definition of the organization of lasting peace than if you had never opened your mouth. These matters belong to the tradition of secret diplomacy and exclusive sovereignties. In dealing with peace in terms of them you have, if the foregoing analyses mean anything at all, only scotched the snake of war, not killed it. The fact is that there exists a stock of commonplaces so obvious, so inevitable to the very simplest act of coöperation between men, that we are not aware of them until they are undermined or hurt. Then we regard them as miraculous novelties and make a great to-do about their application. They are like the air we breathe — a thing we are not conscious

of until our breathing gets troubled —
whereupon we cast about for patent medi-
cines when all we need to do is open the
window. Organizing lasting peace is only
opening the international window.

Organizing lasting peace is only making
deeper, wider and more thoroughgoing application of the irreduceable principles
which are the trite and living foundations
of any and all community life. They have
been known and repeated since the days of
Isaiah and of Plato. They are basic assumptions of this book; only the language
that expresses them has altered, not they.
In toto, they come to some such thing as
this: Men live in families, herds or groups
of varying inheritance, character and organization. To survive and to grow, they
stand in need of food, clothing, shelter and
freedom for the free play of their spontaneous energies. These they obtain by
mastering the non-human natural environment in which they live, by tilling and
mining the soil, harnessing the winds and
the waters, domesticating and hunting the
animals, learning to know and to control the

hidden laws and forces of nature. The tools whereby they win to such competence as is possible to them are the religions, sciences and arts which taken together compose the institutions of civilizations. Now what they cannot in fact master or in fact use, they seek to own. Ownersip consists, in the vast majority of cases, in a restraint upon your fellow from using what you cannot use yourself. Thus, no matter where or what the group may be or how it starts; within it, the tools and materials of life are or become in a short time the private possession of a few peoples and of a few individuals among those peoples. Within nations this situation constitutes the injustices and inequalities of classes and masses, rich and poor, patricians and plebs. Between nations it constitutes the injustices of empires and hegemonies.

A very extensive phase of history then becomes the attempt of the expropriated to recover a control over the necessities of life, a chance for freedom, and a hope for happiness. What we call the principles of democracy and nationality is simply a shorthand sign for this endeavor. Its success is marked by the socialization of what is regarded as private, by the application of the principle of "eminent domain" — the substitution of the rule of law, which is only force made impersonal, for the rule of force, which is only law taken by the individual into his own hands. It is for this reason that, between states, exclusive sovereignty has invariably meant international anarchy; equalization of sovereignty, international peace. As, for the peace within the nation, there is the law before which all men are equal, so for the peace between nations there must be a law before which all nations are equal. Such an equality does not mean similarity. On the contrary, such an equality means the opportunity for each natural human group to liberate, to develop, and to perfect its spontaneous natural differences from its fellows. The cases of the Irish in the British commonwealth and of the Poles under Prussian rule will aptly illustrate how these principles of community and equality apply.

Fifty years ago Ireland was a landlord-ridden country with a terribly exploited and miserable agricultural population. It was a population overtaxed, underfed, and hunted, Catholic in religion yet paying tithes to the Protestant Episcopal Church. It was without opportunity for decent education, without means or help wherewith it could preserve and study and develop the Irish language and literature and the other contents of the Gaelic culture. In 1869 essential reform began. The Protestant Episcopal Church was disestablished and disendowed; the expropriation of the landlord and the establishment of the Irish peasant was begun, and the government with its law and its credit has ever since stood behind the latter against the landlord. It initiated and is still carrying on a great housing reform; it gave aid to home industries; it made local self-government universal; it created a department of agriculture and technical instruction for the whole island; it established and endowed the Irish National University, with its headquarters in Dublin and with colleges in Cork and Galway; it made knowledge of the Irish language obligatory for entrance. This language, because it was the speech of the poor and the miserable, began with the coming of prosperity to be abandoned by the Irish in favor of English. The event follows the definite law of imitation which governs such matters. This law operates in precisely the same way in the United States, where immigrants abandon their mother-tongues for that of the English-speaking upper classes. The politicians of Ireland noted the process but gave no heed to it. When the Irish Renaissance came, when the Gaelic League was organized, it was not the politicians but the British Government that endowed its endeavors, and endowed the teaching of Irish in the public schools. Indeed, since 1901 the government has paid about $60,-000 a year from the Imperial funds for these purposes — twice what was collected in the same period from voluntary contributions in Ireland and the rest of the world. The result: four million Irishmen, mostly small farmers, have lent the British government very nearly $250,000,000 since the war broke out. The Irish Renaissance has added to Ireland's physical as well as spiritual stature. Home Rule is here an issue beside the point, and even that depends on the free will of the Irish to decide how they will have it and then to have the decency to abide by their own decisions. No one of course would pretend that the Irish problem is solved. The significance of the situation is in the fact that the establishment of equality before the law for the Irish has liberated the Irishman, given him at any rate the beginnings of prosperity, and made him loyal to the British commonwealth and the war to the extent of almost a quarter of a billion of dollars.

Now consider Prussian Poland: the Prussian policy has offered the Poles the alternative of extirpation or Prussianization. For a score of years the Prussian government spent $5,000,000 annually trying to buy out the Polish landowners; and failing that, enacted repressive statutes; and finally, in 1908, passed a law providing for the compulsory expropriation of Polish landowners who would not Prussianize.

Although the Treaty of Vienna definitely provided for religious and cultural freedom for the Poles that then came under Prussian dominion, the use of Polish at public meetings is prohibited. Since 1873 German alone may be taught in the national schools; teachers, under a decree of 1899, may not speak Polish in their own homes. Teaching the language and possessing Polish literature are crimes punishable with imprisonment. The Poles are unequal before the law, and the attitude of their rank and file (many of the "nobility" find themselves in a most congenial setting) toward Prussia expresses the inequality. As Plato points out in the first book of the "Republic," there must be honor even among thieves if thieves are to make common cause against honest men. How much the more amongst honest men if they are to live in freedom and safety! And that the system of exclusive sovereignties makes every nation think of every other nation as a thief, he who runs may read in history. Only if the common bases of the common life, only if the world's highways, harbors, raw materials, and undeveloped lands are possessed and used in common, only if a violation of community can be swiftly and adequately punished, can peoples be free for the life and the pursuit of the happiness appropriate to each according to its kind. In a word we require no political nostrums to secure lasting peace. We need only shift our attention, and profit by our own example. We need only open the national windows.

How may this be done? Well, turn to the conduct of the war itself, particularly to its failures, for answer. In the past three years there have arisen occasions when complete military victory might perhaps have been attained by the armies of Democracy. Such victory is indispensable, and we must go on fighting until it is won; we must go on killing yet more and more of the most hopeful and bravest of our blood, and leaving more and more of the future in the hands of men too old for preoccupation with anything but the past, in the hands of backward-looking men. Why? Because, in truth, though the democracies have been fighting a single enemy, they have not been fighting a single war. Between Russia and Ru-

mania, between Italy and Serbia, even between France and Russia, between England
and France, there have been conflicts of
desire toward ownership. Each nation was
fighting first for its own ends, then for the
common end. Lacking a common end,
there could not be a common front; lacking a common front, there could not be
final victory. So our soldiers paid and our
workers paid for the illusion of exclusive
sovereignty. So they will continue to pay
unless the precarious alliance of the democracies is turned into a real one, into a genuine international organization. It took
the defeat of Rumania, the disintegration
of Russia, the Italian débâcle to teach us
this. And we have still much to learn.
And if the whole truth were known, as it
will be known, we have also much to teach.
Never has a nation entered a war with more
unselfish and high-minded purpose than the
United States. Never, under such circumstances has one been more disillusioned by
the greed, selfishness, political traditionalism
and disingenuousness of the governments of
some of its Allies. Our men and our means

have been begged for and commanded, our
ideals have in effect been flouted and denied.
We have been met by diplomacy instead of
honesty, evasion instead of straightforward
Yea and *Nay*. It is not merely to the
peoples of the Central Empires that President Wilson addresses himself over the
heads of governments. This war is a
people's war, and the peoples of the world
will need to be their own saviors. The old
men of the old school who govern them are
incapable by habit and vocation of anything
except betraying them into the hands of the
old system of which this war is the noblest
offspring. Yes, the democracies have still
much to learn. As Norman Angell has
pointed out again and again, military victory is indispensable, but not sufficient.
Only the mobilization of the public opinion
of the democracies in behalf of a democratic
and lasting peace can actually establish such
a peace. The needed mobilization requires
common understanding and assent between
the democratic powers, particularly between the powers of the West and Russia.
The President's message of January 8 rec-

ognized this necessity in clear and vigorous terms. It is a commentary on our other Allies as well as on Russia.* Prostrate in a military sense as Russia seems to be, she has been so far the foremost saving and constructive factor for democracy in the whole international situation.

To those who have been following the political history of Europe since the German assault upon civilization began, it must be clear that the Russian revolution has not merely overturned Czardom and its bureaucracy; it has seriously shaken the whole war-breeding structure of secret diplomacy among the Allies. It upset the arrangements of the misguided Paris Conference; it strengthened liberalism in England, France, and Germany; the Bolshevik pub-

---

*"The conception of what is right, of what it is humane and honorable for them to accept, has been stated with a frankness, a largeness of view, a generosity of spirit and a universal human sympathy which must challenge the admiration of every friend of mankind: and they have refused to compound their ideals or desert others that they themselves may be safe. They call to us to say what it is that we desire, and I believe that the people of the United States would wish me to respond with utter simplicity and frankness. The treatment accorded to Russia by her sister nations in the months to come will be the acid test of their good will, of their comprehension of her need as distinguished from their own interests, and of their intelligent and unselfish sympathy."

lication of dynastic treaties shamed into withdrawal and retirement the ruling Tories who had made them; the Bolshevik negotiations with the Central Powers have now exposed the duplicity of the German government and have farther deepened the gulf between the government and the German people. Lord Lansdowne's magnificent if not disinterested protest was made possible by the Bolsheviki. Of these the leaders are neither captains of industry nor statesmen. They are not trained to do business nor to conduct governments. None the less, they are the masters of both affairs and politics. They are the masters of both because they are possessed of a conviction concerning them, a conviction which is the same time an ideal. This they will not and cannot compromise with any consideration of practicality or fact. It is in the deepest and fullest sense a religious conviction. It involves a vision of evil and sin and an infallible programme of salvation therefrom. It has, among its devotees, its heroes and its martyrs, and it projects upon its deniers, the infidels, the *bourgeoisie,* the misbelievers,

[127]

a ruthless and terrible inquisition. The sin it proclaims is capitalism, is the class war wherein the proletarian masses are constantly being expropriated and enslaved. This sin is the substance of modern civilization and everything else — nationality, imperialism, democracy — is attributive and secondary. Salvation from this sin is socialism. It requires a last judgment, the "social revolution," and the inheritance of the earth by the poor and the meek everywhere. The watchwords of this revolution are "the turn of the wheel," "the rule of the downtrodden." To it all other matters are irrelevant. Finland, Poland, the Ukraine, Siberia, Bessarabia, Lithuania, all the different peoples of the Russian land declare their independence, and it is conceded them. But it is no sooner conceded than the Red Guard is sent to awaken the proletarian revolution among them. Peace on earth, goodwill to men, is the officially proclaimed programme: to achieve it *bourgeoisie* and Jews (Jews are *bourgeoisie* by definition among the Marxists) are expropriated and slaughtered with the rigid impartial logic characteristic of true religion everywhere. On the other hand, unarmed men are sent to their death in the camps of the enemy, to preach "the turn of the wheel." Even while peace negotiations are being conducted with the masters of the German people, the people themselves are being urged to rebellion, urged with a divine and childlike faith in the will and the power of that unhappy people to rise against its masters. The army is demobilized even as peace negotiations are abandoned because the demands of Germans require surrender of the principles of the Revolution. A Constituent Assembly is forcibly dissolved and a " tyranny of the proletariat" forcibly established, to save the Revolution. Peace, on shameful terms, is accepted to save the Revolution, and notice is at the same time served that the real war, the class war, goes on. All this is the logical consequence of a theory of life held as a religion. Acting exclusively on this theory, as on any theory, is acting in a vacuum, consistently, but irrelevantly. Because the Bolsheviki disregard time, place, circumstance and the sinister character of the enemy they are dealing with, they are dooming themselves to failure, Russia to the domination of what to a socialist talking in the symbols of Christianity, is anti-Christ. But faith is of the eternal. They have waited a generation, these Bolsheviki, they have schemed and plotted for a generation; if need be they will wait and scheme and plot as long again. The failure of the faith is only temporary and immediate. Its victory is only postponed. The dark forces of Germany are more afraid of the Bolshevik idea than they were of the Tzarist army. "No propaganda" is their fundamental peace term. And they are wise in their own interest. That propaganda is a religion, and the war has rendered the minds and hearts of the masses of men sensitive and yearning for a liberation just such as it is the evangel of. Persecution and resistance can serve only to strengthen and to spread it. Already it has led to proletarian violence in Germany and in Austria, while its gospel has spread from Brest-Litovsk to the democracies of the world. So the religiously uncompromising adherence to the

[130]

international position by the leaders of the Bolsheviki has thrown the preponderance of influence at last with the plain people of Europe. Without it, the second of the great constructive formations of the war, the new British Labor Party, on which most of all America must count for the support of its international ideals, could not have been encouraged to announce so radical a programme; without it the statements of Lloyd George and President Wilson would hardly have been forthcoming. The Bolsheviki most of all have helped to make the war not only a war for democracy, but a war at last of democracy and by democracy.

For when the war began, the Tories everywhere got into the saddle. They were the men of affairs and enterprise, accustomed to dealing efficiently with large matters. They controlled, as they still are controlling in this country, men and material to please themselves. The masses of the people were only to feel, to pay taxes, and to serve in army and factory. The masses of the people everywhere did so willingly and happily. Labor gave up its

rights, and intellect its necessary prerogative; and a heyday of profiteering, tax-
dodging, and bitter-endism began. But the
people soon grew restive. England and
France changed the incidence of taxation;
their governments deferred more and more
to the condition of labor, though not to its
position. Liberalism and intelligence were
everywhere censored and repressed. Secret
diplomacy prevailed; the obvious will of
the people to a just and democratic and
lasting peace was ignored. An abyss de-
veloped between peoples and governments,
an abyss which Lloyd George's address to
the Labor Party closed in England, but
which the intransigeant attitude of Clemen-
ceau widens in France. Governments,
speaking for the future of capital, saw peace
in the old terms of diplomatic deceit.
Peoples, war weary, hungry for freedom
and happiness, saw peace in the new terms
of a commonwealth of nations. Friction
and unrest began to show themselves, with
one terminus in the Rumanian débâcle and
another in the Italian disaster. Mean-
while came the Russian revolution and the

fear of it and revulsion against it by the
Tories, embattled everywhere but in the
trenches, where Toryism cannot survive.
Accusations, condemnations — everything
that the interests who saw their preroga-
tives threatened thereby could hurl, was
hurled against the Revolution. At the same
time events in Russia took their inevitable
course. Two provisional governments
that failed to execute the deep-lying will
of the Russian people for a just, democratic
and lasting peace disintegrated and dis-
appeared in much smoke and some blood.
The history of the present Bolshevik administration merits all that President Wilson said of it, and much more. Although it
cannot last, it is while it does last the one
fertilizing force that throughout Europe is
making governments answerable to peoples.
By its mere being it is forcing an extension
of the scope of democracy not less in England than in Rumania and Austria and
Germany.

The one country where it has not this
effect is the United States. The reasons are
not too ambiguous. President Wilson at

least — I will not say our government —
has an international vision coincident with
the Russians'. The very causes that brought
us into the war throw together the hopes of
the two democracies. And so " the government " of the United States has from the
beginning stood by the new Russia with
men, material, and opinion; and it has in
this carried out the will of the American
people. But the vocal class of our country,
the class that controls the press, that is
amassing fortunes because of the war, that
resists equitable taxation such as our allies
have ordained, that is administratively in
the saddle, and that demands the (to it)
profitable establishment of permanent and
universal military service — this class has
opposed that coöperation. It has done all
it could, by denunciation and what not, to
destroy the understanding, precarious at
best, between Russia and the United States.
So has it given aid and comfort to the
enemy. It has strengthened the morale of
the enemy by creating materials that the
enemy government could use in urging the
German people to go on fighting in "self-

defence." It has used patriotism as a cloak for partisanship, and national loyalty for local advantage. It has been loud in denouncing freedom of speech and of the press. In Russia this class, the Junker and ruling class, has been heard and discussed far more than any other American class. To the Russian democracy they are America, and unless the democracy of America makes itself heard as the democracy of England has made itself heard they will remain America. Today it is not believed in Russia that President Wilson will be able to carry out that wise programme of war aims, restated upon the demand of the democracy of Russia. Only the action of American labor, in common with all our country's other liberal forces, discussing and endorsing these aims, can awaken that belief. Only the action of labor, in common with all our country's other liberal forces, in demanding and helping to create an international machinery, can make that belief secure. Such action will render democratic and lasting peace inevitable. It will enable the democratic allies to reap the full benefit of military victory because it will detach the German people from the German government. It is an action that must be taken at once, in common with the workingmen of England, France, Italy, and Russia. It means getting efficiently behind our President at home and holding up the hands of our soldiers abroad.

But how is such action to be taken? What is to be asked for and how is it to be obtained? All the peace conferences that have ever been, have been held by diplomats under appointment and behind closed doors. How can the forthcoming conference be held otherwise? There is no precedent.

But there is a precedent, and a precedent that is absolute in similarity. It is to be found in the history of our own country. We do not regard it as a precedent, because we have come to think of the United States of America as one nation. But between 1776 and 1787 the thirteen independent and sovereign states that underwent the American Revolution were in precisely the same position and confronted precisely the same problems, in principle, as the present states and governments of the world. They won through to a combination of interstate unity with state sovereignty from which we benefit today. And all that this combination amounts to is the equality of states before interstate law. There is far less reason why the peoples and states concerned in the present war should not win through, and by methods analogous or the same, to an analogous end.

IX

THE FEDERALIZATION OF SOVEREIGN STATES: A PRECEDENT NOT ACCORDING TO INTERNATIONAL LAW

IX

THE FEDERALIZATION OF SOVEREIGN STATES: A PRECEDENT NOT ACCORDING TO INTERNATIONAL LAW

THE thirteen original British colonies in America, united against the aggressive exploitation of the British government, differed in one fundamental respect from the free states today in alliance against Germany: they had no " problems of nationality." By and large, they were of one blood, one language, and one legal and political tradition. That this did not prevent bitter quarrels and even warfare among them is only another evidence that nationality, even when sovereign, is not the antidote to warfare its contemporary protagonists assert it is. Men go to war from other motives as well, and the phenomenon of two states of the same nationality at each other's throats is not so infrequent in history that it may be ignored. Members of the thirteen colonies were at each other's throats for a variety of reasons, religious and economic, and it was only the menace of a common enemy that at first drew and held them together. They came together as "sovereign and independent states," reluctantly, strongly suspicious of one another and inclined to act each in its own behalf. To meet an enemy strong, well armed, and well supplied, they had to provide an army with all that an army needs for effective effort in the field. And they had to create this provision out of practically nothing at all, to secure the very finances with which to create. From the beginning each state held to its right to perform its share of this work for itself and as it chose, without regard for, or any attempt at coöperation with, the other states. From the beginning each state failed to do its proper share, out of fear, largely, that it might be doing more than its share; and each state, correspondingly, complained of the inefficiency of the central authority, the Continental Congress. But the Congress was in effect a consulting and advisory body, becoming negligible through inaction, and doomed to inaction because it was without real power. The war, indeed, was not truly one war but many wars, and the remoter states were colder to the issues and conditions of the conflict than those at its seat. These issues and conditions were the inevitable ones of finance, of the control of the food-supply, of the army commissariat. The lack of common action and unified authority on these points caused untold suffering to the soldiers and indefinitely prolonged the struggle.

To secure the necessary unity the Congress had discussed for a year and finally submitted to the legislatures of the states articles of a confederation without which the war could not successfully be carried on. These articles did not win final ratification till 1781. They were accompanied by a circular letter the following extract from which is relevant:

The business [of unification], equally intricate and important, has in its progress been attended with uncommon embarrassments and delay, which the most anxious solicitude and persevering diligence could not prevent. To form a permanent union, accommodated to the opinion and wishes of the delegates of so many states differing in habits, produce, commerce, and internal police, was found to be a work with which nothing but time and reflection, *conspiring with a disposition to conciliate* [italics mine] could mature and accomplish.

Hardly is it to be expected that any plan, in the variety of provisions essential to our union, should exactly correspond with the maxims and political views of every particular state. Let it be remarked that, after the most careful inquiry and the fullest information, this is proposed as the best which could be adapted to the circumstances of all, and as that alone which affords any tolerable prospect of general satisfaction.

The Articles of Confederation were primarily a war measure, designed to make the efforts of many sovereign states effective against one common enemy. They were by second intention an instrument of security between the states themselves, designed to maintain lasting peace between them and to strengthen each with all and all with each. They provided therefore that the states were to retain all undelegated sovereignty; that they were to constitute an absolute military unity against the enemy assaulting any one of them; that the citizens of one, moving to another, were to receive equal treatment with the citizens of that other; that each should have equal authority with the others, large or small, on the basis of one state, one vote; that no state might enter into special relations with another, or with a foreign power, except by general consent; that no state might ordain a tariff at cross-purposes with the general interest; that Congress alone, representing the general interest, might determine the armament of each state; that no state might go to war except by general consent; that hence treaties, alliances, the making of war and peace were to be the functions of Congress; that Congress was to be the " last resort on appeal on all differences now subsisting or that hereafter may arise between two or more states concerning boundary, jurisdiction, or any other cause whatsoever." Its proceedings were to be publicly recorded in a journal to be kept for that purpose. The Articles provided, please observe, for all the contingencies that liberal opinion finds it desirable to guard against in the relations between contemporary states.

They are a programme of international-ism. Under them the Revolutionary War dragged out to a successful conclusion. But with the coming of peace the force of the international authority, of the Congress they provided for, lapsed altogether. The states reverted to their aboriginal sover-eignty, and worse. The central authority carried an enormous burden of debt, the states were destitute, the country disorgan-ized. Patriotism, that is, local loyalties of the peoples to their different state govern-ments, was intense.

The mutual antipathies and clashing interests of the Americans, their difference of govern-ments, habitudes, and manners [wrote Josiah Tucker] indicate that they will have no center of union and no common interest. They can never be united into one compact empire under any species of government whatever; a dis-united people till the end of time, suspicious and distrustful of each other, they will be divided and subdivided into little common-wealths or principalities, according to natural boundaries, by great bays of the sea, and by vast rivers, lakes, and ranges of mountains.

Add dynastic and national interests, and the description absolutely dots the present and future of both the powers within the democratic alliance and those opposed to it.

But the Dean of Gloucester was mistaken. The situation he described, the unnecessary length and hardship of the war, the horrible civil blunders never would have arisen at all if the Articles of Confederation had made Congress truly authoritative and had provided it with power to enforce its ordinances. Its power unfortunately was like that of the Hague Tribunal, purely advisory: "They may declare everything," wrote Justice Story, " but can do nothing." Only the presence of the common enemy kept Congress in force during the war. With the coming of peace, not only did its power tend to lapse; it was scorned, and the several states treated it with the suspicion due an encroaching foreigner. "The Confederation was," according to J. Q. Adams, " perhaps as closely knit together as it was possible that such a form of polity could be grappled; but it was matured by the State Legislatures *without consultation with the people* [the italics are mine] and the jealousy of sectional collisions and the distrust of all delegation of power, stamped every feature of the work with inefficiency." Mr. Adams hit upon the very heart of the difficulty. The Confederation was a thing made by statesmen and diplomats. Reputable though they were, their mere authority could not win for it the allegiance of the masses, and without that it could have no force. Had the masses been instructed by discussion and analysis, and had public opinion been awakened to reënforce the obviously wise programme, the history of these United States would have been otherwise written.

Because public opinion had not been roused, the removal of enemy pressure was followed by a reversion to pre-war conditions, aggravated by the disabling consequences of the war. The separate states at once began to act upon the traditional principle that a government's safety depends upon its own strength and its neighbors' weakness. Tariff war began almost immediately. Various ententes and alliances were initiated. Massachusetts tried to detach the other New England states into a separate union. New York went to war with Vermont, which had declared its independence of New Hampshire, over the strip of Vermont settled by New Yorkers and paying taxes to New York. Maryland and Virginia organized a sort of *zollverein* which Delaware and Pennsylvania were later invited to join. It did seem as if the threatened disintegration of the Confederation were inevitable. One thing held it together and kept for Congress such authority as remained to it. This was the public domain. Prior to the confederation the various states had held or claimed enormous reaches of territory, stretching to the Mississippi or beyond. (These territories correspond to the African possessions of today's warring states.) Maryland's refusal to confederate until all the holdings of the states should be surrendered to the common authority compelled the pooling of these lands, and the lands pooled thereupon became the national domain. The domain constituted a tangible obvious interstate interest and was in effect the cornerstone of the Union.

At the same time, the best minds in all of the states — not those in Congress but those that had the respect of the masses — were agitated by the difficulties of the situation. The problems that needed adjustment were precisely those that so largely need adjustment today, the problems of international commerce and finance, of the common highways of trade, of tariffs, of undeveloped territories. Their solution, it was recognized, required an *effective* easement upon the exclusive sovereignty of each state. The initiation of the Maryland-Virginia *zollverein* was an attempt at such an easement with respect to a vital matter, analogous in contemporary Europe to the internationalization of the Danube. The movement to include all the states in an extension of this arrangement led to the Constitutional Convention, an " assembly of demigods" that owed its existence as much to the self-sacrifice and initiative of the non-administrative leaders of political thought in the country as to the action of the state legislatures. These leaders created the Constitution and with it the United States of America.

Now there are many strictures to be made upon the Constitution. It is undoubtedly the instrument of the conservers of the powers and privileges of property that Charles Beard says it is. And it is deserving of all the other objections that have been leveled at it. Nevertheless, it has designated for the states that have put themselves under its rule the structure of lasting peace. That it did not do so absolutely, that in spite of it we underwent a Civil War, is acknowledged. Had the framers of the Constitution been more courageously true to their convictions, that disaster need not have befallen us. But with respect to the elimination of basic causes of war between nations the Constitution is definitive.

In this definitiveness it does not, however, surpass the Articles of Confederation. Those delimit more precisely the possibilities within the will and the effective reach of mankind today. Add to them the necessary power to enforce this common will, and you have provided, not absolute insurance against war, but a structure that will progressively make war less and less likely. Force is the greatest need. To begin anything new, to break an old habit, to depart from a custom or a tradition requires first of all the will so to act, but it requires most of all, force. The insurance of lasting peace is force, generalized into law. The fundamental task of those concerned about the permanence of peace, is to secure, and to provide for the uses of, such force.

X

THE FEDERALIZATION OF SOVEREIGN STATES: PRELIMINARIES, CONDITIONS, AND PRINCIPLES OF A LEAGUE OF NATIONS

X

THE FEDERALIZATION OF SOVEREIGN STATES: PRELIMINARIES, CONDITIONS, AND PRINCIPLES OF A LEAGUE OF NATIONS

TO three causes is to be attributed the failure of the Articles of Confederation between the thirteen original and sovereign states in the American Union. The most important was the fact that the Confederation's central authority, its Congress, had no power; and it had no power because it had no support in public opinion, the citizens of the states being inordinately jealous of the exclusive sovereignty of their respective states. Again, the failure of public opinion to " get behind " the Congress was due to the fact that it had been created by an administrative fiat of the State Legislatures, without any reference whatsoever to such opinion. Hence the existence and function of Congress were without contact with the immediate life and interests of the people from whose interest and consent power, in that instance, derived. The three causes were at bottom one: *Congress could not enforce its rulings.* How to secure for it this force was the crucial problem before the Constitutional Convention, and the advance which the instrument framed by that body made over the Articles of Confederation is to be measured solely by the degree of power it put into the hands of the Federal agencies of government.

At the present writing the relationships of the democratic nations echo those of the American states between 1776 and 1787. What unity they have is enforced by the presence of a common enemy. The hypertrophied passion for exclusive sovereignty which is the vicious side of patriotism, and the drag of a diplomatic technique determined by the interests of such sovereignty have rendered genuinely federated action on a single front unnecessarily difficult. Arrangements between the allied democracies are separate arrangements and their character is that of treaty, not of public law. When Mr. Lloyd George, compelled by events to denounce the inexcusable *impasse* which this had led the Allies into, made his famous demand for unification, this jealousy — instinctive, animal — for the integrity of the herd, led to a vicious and unjustified assault upon him. Withal, the degree of coöperation between the democratic allies is tremendously greater than was that between the American states. But here again, the moving cause is not the will of statesmen; the moving cause is the character of a warfare dependent upon the nature and necessities of industrial society. The organization of industrial life has changed warfare from an affair of armies to an affair of nations: the logic of social circumstance and of industrial machinery has compelled a federalization far beyond the present good will of rulers. Were the statesmen of the democratic alliance intelligent and courageous and free enough to follow out immediately what events will force them to concede ultimately, as the inevitable implications of this logic, a constitutional convention would now be in public session for the federation of Russia, England, France, the United States, the South American republics, China, and Japan and our other allies. It would be in session, war or no war, and it would generalize the present practices of coöperation, integrate them, and enact them into law, with the doors open for the Central Powers to come in or not, as they chose.

Such far-seeing relevancy in international conduct is not, however, to be hoped for. Everything international will be postponed until the peace conference; and if we may trust the tone of the ruling and possessing classes, it is a bold aspiration to hope that the compulsion of industrial interdependence and the impulsion of the very patent will of the peoples of Europe and America to a league of nations and a democratic and lasting peace will find their realization and satisfaction even then.

It is a bold aspiration. For the undercurrents of industry and the streams of feeling run counter to the conscious life, the established habits, and the avowed purposes of the rulers of men. Those are dominated by precedents from simpler, more dynastic, mercantile, less popular times; by ideals of "self-sufficient" states bargaining with their peers for advantage, regardless of peoples. But states are no longer self-sufficient, and cannot be. The machine has destroyed their sovereignty even at its most vital point. The machine has destroyed the individuality of the worker also at its vital point, and because, by force of it, seventeen men make the thing that one man used to make without it, the seventeen men have become as one, and are learning to think their needs, their interests, and their purposes as one. It is these needs, interests, and purposes that compose the undercurrents of industry and streams of collective feeling. Woe to the diplomacy that does not regard them! They make the popular will, and this popular will needs only to be clarified by discussion and articulated in a definite programme. Diplomacy everywhere, however, has denounced discussions as "disloyal" or "unpatriotic," and programmes as "visionary." The *Realpolitiker* of the public press and the interests it guards have had very little good

to say of Mr. Wilson's address of January 8;
yet they have not said the worst thing that
there is to be said about it. That worst
thing is this: It puts the cart before the
horse, and the cart is only the skeleton of
a cart. The article requiring a league of
nations should have come first, not last; and
it should have been a definite programme
for the organization of such a league, not
a statement that a league is desirable. The
will of the peoples to enduring peace needs
such a programme to integrate it — a programme that shall designate the personnel
of the peace conference and the manner of
their election; the organization of the conference into a congress; and the chief
articles in an international agreement, such
as shall come home to the vital interests of
the masses of men and women everywhere.

Why the constitution of a league of nations ought to be the first proposition in
the agenda of the peace conference should
be obvious enough. Once certain principles
of public law are established, the adjudica-
tion of all specific racial, territorial, economic, and military issues will follow easily

and smoothly enough from them. The converse is not true. Let these issues be taken up severally and separately, without regard to an international rule, and the peace conference will become a bargain counter between dickering diplomats representing military forces. The specific adjudications will preclude a general principle which must necessarily contradict them. At best we shall have restored a precarious balance of power; at worst we shall resume fighting. If the peace conference be permitted to begin at the wrong end of the series of problems, there is little hope for a good end to the conference.

Whether or not the end it begins at is right will depend on two factors. These are the pressure of enlightened public opinion upon it and the personnel of the conference itself. The former must be awakened by free discussion; the latter will be determined by the manner of their choice and the considerations leading to it. In this regard the experience of the "sovereign and independent" American states is illuminating. At the Constitutional Convention the only statesman who had also been a member of the Continental Congress that had conducted the war against England, was James Madison. The rest were the "demigods" who had won the confidence of the citizens of their states through very specific and signal service during the war or through intellectual leadership during and after it. So now. Diplomatists are by training, habit, and usage unfit for the particular service in hand. Servants of international conflict for exclusive national advantage, their skill is only in the arts of innuendo and dickering which such service demands. They would be as unsuited to a task requiring frankness and mutual accommodation as a pork-magnate to settle a strike in his own packing plant. The men needed are the men of international mind, who have been studying these diplomatists in action, who are aware of the defects of the present state system, and who have thought out alterations and improvements. Such men are Sidney Webb, Brailsford, Henderson, Lowes-Dickinson, Norman Angell in England; Thomas and his fellow

Socialists in France; the members of the present Russian government and innumerable others in Russia; John Dewey, Louis Brandeis, Secretary Baker, David Starr Jordan, and Thorstein Veblen in America; and so in every country. Representatives should be chosen from the effective leadership of that great body of sentiment and opinion which has for the last quarter of a century kept the creation of a league of nations and the establishment of lasting peace constantly before the minds of men, which has so taught these ideals that the present war is unique in that the democratic urge to see it through to victory is the world-wide community of sentiment and opinion against all war. In short, a league of nations can be most effectively established only by representatives who are for it by habit of mind as well as desire, who have given it prolonged study, and have made themselves expert in the programmes of its inauguration.

But there is yet a further necessity in the delimitation of personnel. " Self-determination " for nationalities, sincerely applied, would give place and voice in the conference to representatives of all nationalities whose fate and status the conference is to decide. An autonomous Poland, for example, is undoubtedly desirable, but the unspeakable Polish overlords maintain a vicious hegemony over Lithuanians, Letts, and Jews, no less than over Polish peasants. Lithuanians, Letts, and Jews as well as Poles should have voice and place at the peace conference. Serbo-Croats, Bohemians, Poles, Rumans should represent Austria no less than Magyars and Germans. Arabs, Armenians, Kurds, to mention just a few, should have voice and place equally with the Osmanli Turks, for the Ottoman empire. How the representatives of the minorities are to be elected, what their proportionate weight should be, are questions to be solved by the judgment of experts tested by free discussion and public opinion. That the cases for their peoples must be put by the chosen representatives of these peoples, that they must necessarily have a voice in deciding their own fate in the community of nations, is beyond argument.

[164]

So much so indeed that, following the principle involved, Mr. Norman Angell suggests the representation not alone of nationalities but also of political parties within nations according to their numerical strength. Thus Germany would be represented by her Socialists as well as by the party in power, England by her Laborites as well as by her Liberals and Conservatives, and so on. In this way fundamental differences in political principle would get representation, no less than differences in national character and interest. A real Congress of nations would come into existence.

What the peace conference defining itself as such a Congress would need to establish is the principle of a minimum genuine international control.

Now all political control consists in the exercise of two functions. One is limitation; the other, liberation. Limitation and liberation are distinct but not different, since every just and relevant limitation is a liberation — witness the traffic policeman. International limitation would apply to national armaments, to quarrels between states over the " stakes of diplomacy," to quarrels within states over national hegemonies.

The limitation of armament is of course basic. For no matter what may be the provocation to a fight, the lack of weapons compels the substitution of persuasion for blows and fundamentally alters the locus and sensibility of the "national honor," a figment, if we may trust Mr. Roosevelt as well as history, for the defence of which most blows are struck. Hence the International Congress should determine for the nations of the world, as the Continental Congress was by the Articles of Confederation empowered to determine for the original thirteen American States, the extent of the armament of each state. The simplest way to do this would be to fix annually the amount of money each state might spend on armament. Control of expenditure would require the complete socialization of the manufacture of munitions, its subjection to inspection and control by an international commission on armaments, and absolute publicity of records and accounts. All uses of armament should require license from the International Congress, particularly such uses as go by the euphemism "punitive expedition." Failure to carry out these provisions or to submit to the rule of the International Congress should be regarded tantamount to a declaration of war.

It should be so regarded with respect to the other causes of quarrel between and within states. Interstate disputes of whatever nature should be submitted to the International Congress, which would be also the highest and final court. There has been a good deal of silly differentiation between "justiciable" and "non-justiciable" disputes, but there's nothing that's one or the other but thinking makes it so. All group disputes are justiciable if public opinion says they are. And what public opinion says depends on what it wishes, and what it wishes on what it knows, and what it knows on the degree it has been enlightened by education and publicity. When the International Congress has passed on any dispute, it is settled. Failure to accept the decision of the Congress should automatically constitute a challenge of international power and be dealt with accordingly.

The devices for dealing with such failure are not exclusively military. The military machine, indeed, should be the last resort. Initially, there is the tremendous force of public opinion, which the Church wielded in the Middle Ages as the Excommunication and the Interdict. These should be revived. The economic, social, cultural, or total ostracism of states or portions of states involves tremendously less hardship and suffering than actual military assault and in the long run is bound in an industrial society like ours to attain the same end, far more than in earlier, less interdependent ones.

What degree of coercive power these provisions would have at the outset will depend of course on the will of the signatories to any international constitution not to turn it into a scrap of paper. This will would be embodied in joint military or social action or both, against violators of international law as uttered in the decisions

of the Congress. The governmental organs
of such public will can be regulated, let me
repeat, only by the public opinion of each
state, and the public opinion of each state
can be kept internationally minded only by
means of the completest publicity regarding all international relationships. Publicity and education are the cornerstone of
any international system that shall be democratic and efficacious. Hence the rule of
publicity is a paramount limitative rule.

The foregoing provisions would, I think,
supply the coercive force, the lack of which
rendered the American Confederation so
instructive a failure. That they will absolutely prevent war cannot be claimed.
Even the Constitution of the United States
failed to do that, and the interstate unity it
provided for became a permanent constituent of American political common sense
only with the Civil War. No doubt history
on the terrestrial scale will repeat history
on the continental. No doubt there will
occur, as in America, *blocs* and combinations within the combination, nullification
and attempts at dissolution; but there will

[169]

be in constant operation also, as in America, a definitely formulated, agreed-to principle of unity, insuring mankind against a great many wars almost certain to come without it, and ultimately against all wars.

Yet the chief power of this insurance would reside in the function of liberation that the instruments of internationality would perform. Those turn on the satisfaction of the basic wants of men, and the consequent release of their spontaneous energies in the creative activities their natures crave. Such satisfaction and release demand, as we have already seen, a free trade in material commodities at least equivalent to the free trade in things of the spirit—in science, for example, or art, or music. It would be fundamental for the International Congress to create international commissions concerning themselves with the coördination of efforts to increase and properly distribute the food supply, to maintain and improve international health, to maintain and keep internationally open the world's highways, to secure the equality of all men before the law of any land, to expand and intensify the world's sense of community by internationally coördinated education.

Most of these functions have already been forced on the allied democracies by the exigencies of war; they would need only to be made relevant to conditions of peace. Such are the food and fuel administrations, acting purely in view of international needs. Others existed long before the war. Such are the postal union, and Mr. David Lubin's indispensably serviceable agricultural institute, now living a starved life in Italy. Still others have gone on as voluntary and private enterprises. Such are the various learned societies, particularly the medical and the chemical societies. These would need endowment, endorsement, establishment under international rule. In none of these enterprises, please note, is a novel material necessary. All the institutions exist. Attention needs only to be shifted to their coöperative integration, expansion, and perfection by the conscious joint effort of the nations of the world to turn them into a genuine machinery of liberating international government.

The most important instrument of internationality is, however, education. Take care of education, Plato makes Socrates say in the " Republic," and education will take care of everything else. Internationally, education must rest on two principles: one, that it must be autonomous; the other, that it must be unprejudiced.

Regarding the first: We have already seen how, in the case of Germany, the state's control of education laid the foundation for the present war. The school served the state's vested interest in the school as, formerly, it had served that of the Church. From the dark ages to the present day the Church had held a vested interest in the school, an interest from which events have more or less freed the latter but which still makes itself felt. With the rise of private educational institutions or the secularization of theological ones — such as Harvard or Yale or Princeton — with the elaboration of the public school systems of the different states of this country or any other, the powers of government, visible or invisible, have determined largely what should and what should not be taught, what is true and what is false, always from the point of view of the interests of these powers. Heresy has been consistently persecuted, with means varying from the auto-da-fé of the Church to the more delicate tools of contemporary university trustees or school committees. Heresy consists of that which is not in accord with the interests or prejudices of the ruling power.

Now the art of education involves three elements: First, its theme — the growing child, whose creative spontaneities are to be encouraged, whose capacities for service and happiness are to be actualized, intensified, and perfected. Second, the investigator and inventor or artist who discovers or makes the material and machinery which are the conditions of the child's life and growth, which liberate or repress these. Third, the teacher who transmits to the child the knowledge of the nature and use of these things, drawing out its powers and enhancing its vitality by means of them.

Obviously, to the last two, to the discoverers and creators of knowledge, and to its transmitters and distributors, to these and to no one else beside, belongs the control of education. It is as absurd that any but teachers and investigators should govern the art of education as that any but medical practitioners and investigators should govern the art of medicine. International law would best abolish the existing external control by making the communities of educators everywhere autonomous bodies, vigorously cooperative in an international union. Within this union the freest possible movement of teachers and pupils should be provided for by way of exchanges of both between all nationalities to the end of attaining the acme of free trade in habits and theories of life, in letters, and in methods.

Regarding the second principle of internationalized education — that it must be unprejudiced: This requires the systematic internationalization of certain subject-matters. In the end, of course, all subject-matters get internationalized. The process is, however, too slow and too dangerous with respect to some of these, history being the most flagrant. Compare any collection of history text-books with any similar collection in physics, for example, and you will find the latter possessed of a unanimity never to be attained in the former. Why? Because every hypothesis in physics is immediately tested in a thousand laboratories and the final conclusion is the result of the collective enterprise of all sorts and conditions of physicists. In the writing of history such coöperative verification never occurs. Most histories, particularly those put into the hands of children, utter vested interests, not scientifically tested results; they utter sectarian or national vanity, class privilege, class resentment, and so on. Compare any English history of the American Revolution with any American history! Fancy the wide divergence of assertion between friends and enemies in the matter of German atrocities! Naturally, the interpretation of historic " fact " must and should vary with the interpreter, but the designation of the same " fact " should clearly be identical for all interpreters. To keep education unprejudiced requires therefore the objective designation of historic fact — "historic" to mean the recorded enterprise of all departments of human life. The "facts" of history should be attested by an international commission. So the second function of education is served.

With this we have established the full pattern of the house of peace — an international democratic congress, limiting armaments, judging disputes, coördinating and harmonizing the great national institutions by means of which men get food and clothing and shelter and health and happiness, making for a free exchange of all excellence, punishing default with interdict or excommunication or war, resting its authority upon public opinion and strengthening it by internationalized education.

XI

EPILOGUE: HUMAN NATURE AND THE LIMITS OF INTERNATIONALISM

XI

EPILOGUE: HUMAN NATURE AND THE LIMITS OF INTERNATIONALISM

SOLEMN warnings echo through the land. Prophets stalk uncensored, prophesying war and woe unless we arm forever. Solemn warnings flash across the editorial pages of the kept press; and the weighty voices of Colonel Roosevelt and Congressman Kahn, of the National Security League and the munition manufacturers, of professors of international law out of Laputa, and of all the comfortable gentlemen who have passed middle age and are drawing upon a rich experience with life and light and leading, are crying to us, "Arm, arm! or we are lost." What these sapiencies think of human nature is not fit to print.

And the worst of it is, they are not without provocation. Who, looking over the history of human conduct dare say they are? According to the true testimony of history war is an institution of civilization and an invention of man. To say with the militarist philosophy made in Germany that the non-human world lives by war, is a blasphemy against Nature and a libel upon plants and animals. For war is organized murder for non-essential purposes. The struggle for survival is not organized, and it regards essentials only. Animals do not kill for the sake of killing; they kill for food, nor do they kill their own kind. In the botanical world plants do not survive by destroying their rivals; they do not regard their rivals. Plants survive by their own inward vigor, striking roots into the earth and shoots toward the sun. They simply crowd out their rivals by doing better the same things that the rivals are doing.

And this is no less true for the great achievements of mankind. Artists do not seek to destroy each other; they seek to emulate each other by painting better pictures, composing better music or better poems. Scientists do not seek each other's lives. Their rivalry consists in this — that each seeks to achieve more perfectly what the other is doing. The competition between

[180]

men that makes for civilization and progress does not aim to kill the rival, it aims to improve upon the work of the rival. The survival and growth and activity of the rival is an indispensable condition for the improvement of the work. The competition is in fact a coöperation, not a slaughter. And this is true on all levels of human life. The masses of men do not aim to kill one another. Like the plants they do not regard one another. They aim at freedom and happiness. Now war is intentional killing and is common only to a small portion of mankind. The masses of men are driven or persuaded into war and never have undertaken and never would of their own initiative undertake it. War is a class perversion of the universal enterprise of self-expression and self-realization.

As an institution war rests upon the plasticity and inertia of human nature. Upon the plasticity because war must be carried on either by driven slaves or mercenaries or deceived free men, and the war-lust is generated in free men by infection from their rulers. What moves their rulers when these are dynastic is the vanity or the greed of the personage commanding their allegiance; what moves their rulers when these are national states are the same motives, going, however, by the names "national honor" and "the balance of trade." Both demand more than is needful or due for the actual free existence either of princes or states. These are able to infect men with the war-lust, even when the latter realize that war can do them no good whatsoever, because of the inertia of human nature. Men live far more by habit and tradition than by initiative and thought. The habits of deference and obedience to the masters, the reverence for the idols the masters are and for the shibboleths they delude men with, reënforce the initial military infection and plastic responsiveness to the stirred-up herd feeling. Fear also plays its part, fear of rulers, fear of neighbors: German privates are fighting today because they fear their officers more than the enemy; Russian privates are not fighting, because they have ceased to fear their officers. War rests upon and reënforces the maxims "Everybody's doing it" and "What was good enough for father is good enough for me."

That which originates war and spreads it is not, however, that which nourishes it in the mind of the common man. Though it is generated upon the plasticity and inertia in human nature, it is justified by the soul's initiative. The society we live in is basically a system of taboos — taboos set by class for mass, by property for humanity, by civilization for the animal as well as spiritual spontaneities within us. Hence war is to society what drink is to the individual. It dulls the sense of repression, breaks up inhibitions, and liberates and satisfies energies and appetites normally starved. Note that from the point of view of the possessing classes prohibition is suicidal. No doubt it enhances "efficiency"; but the stored-up discontents of workingmen customarily dissipated in the irrelevancies of drink, accumulate under prohibition, and sooner or later must be discharged relevantly, upon the injustices generating these discontents. By prohibition capitalism is digging its own grave. With regard to war, however, its instinct is less blinded by greed. Hence the jeremiads of Mr. Roosevelt and his ilk. In war times there is an exaltation in the land: even civilians are lifted out of themselves as by strong drink; their hatreds, prejudices, malices, and lusts need only to be decently cloaked by patriotism to flourish at the acme of propriety, while in the battlefields — frightfulness, regardless of race or state.

Now it is to be observed that the pressure toward peace and internationalism has been a direct function of the spread of democracy, and the spread of democracy has consisted in the removal of political, economic, superstitious, and social taboos upon the panting energies, the spontaneous creative powers of the masses of men. They have most to gain from lasting peace and internationalism; they have it most in their power to make them real.

Will they do it? Can they do it? The portents are not unfavorable. Men are awake in Russia and in England, and they need but to take thought in France and in Italy and with open minds and active wills

" get behind the President " in America. What is called human nature by the elderly gentlemen who govern the world today and of whose interests and dogmas the Roosevelts and Milners are the high priests, is not human nature at all. What is called human nature by these greedy and backward looking men is only second nature. Civilization is a growth, not an eternal form. Customs, conventions, and habits are things that once were not and that ultimately will not be. Investment too easily identifies these changing manners and morals of society with everlasting law, makes of them idols and masters where they ought to be symbols and servants. The civilization of Europe has gone a long way since the days of the Holy Roman Empire, and what was eternal law then is only superstitious survival now. Change, society does and will, no matter how our wishes and interests may in idea arrest it, holding fast to this or that form or institution. Mankind is aware of this today as never before in its history and because it is so aware of this the question for the modern world has become: Shall we suffer or direct this change? Shall we be its victims or its masters?

There is only one answer in the world so awake as ours to change and self. Human institutions are but the mutual accommodations of distinct if not separate human wills, accommodations unconscious at first but progressively subject to conscious control. Society is more and more what we choose to make it. In the forms of human organization belief *is* fact. "If you will it," said Theodore Herzl, urging his people toward the new Zion, "it is no dream." Surely the record of new achievement and invention in this our world, a record as rich as that of the less conspicuously changing old order which so dominates our attention, is sufficient warrant for attempting a new order which needs no more to make it real than a shift of this same attention. We have changed institutions with unheard-of swiftness in the last century. We have conquered space and time with machines. We have battered down tyranny, superstition and ignorance with knowledge, with revolution, with ideals of freedom, equality and fraternity that have not been absent from the minds of the masses of men from the day they were first uttered to the present hour. Mankind has won for itself in the course of the last century a freedom unparalleled in all the milleniums of recorded history that have gone before. Shall it stay its hand and its hope? It need only to will this new thing, which is merely a new arrangement of old things. Human nature is not in conflict with lasting peace and a free international order. It sets no limits to internationalism. Only the perversion of human nature by the illusions of exclusive sovereignty, the sordid realities of class vanity and class greed, of "national honor" and the "rights of property" limit and combat it. Regard a free league of free peoples: if you will it, it is no dream.